BOY ON A HILL

Memories of childhood and youth in Lincoln between the wars.

by

REG WOODWARD

Illustrated by

DAVID PARKINS

~ She was greatly my superior in both batting and bowling ~

© Reg Woodward 1984

Printed by G. W. Belton Ltd.
Gainsborough
ISBN 0 9509586 0 3

FOREWORD
by
The Dean of Lincoln

It is with great pleasure that I write the foreword to this book, written by an ex-chorister of Lincoln Cathedral. His reminiscences are a fascinating portrayal of how a boy and man of lively interests grew up between the two world wars. He is right when he says that the disciplines of life as a choirboy, 'a child doing a man's work in a man's world'', help boys to be successful in adult life. This book is surely an admirable example of that fact.

Oliver Fiennes

Preface

I feel someone ought to try to record what life was like in my native city fifty years ago and can only echo the prayer of a seventeenth century nun:

"Lord, I dare not ask for improved memory but for a growing humility and a lessening cocksureness when my memory seems to clash with the memories of others. Teach me the glorious lesson that occasionally I may be mistaken".

I should like to express my grateful thanks to the Dean of Lincoln for writing the Foreword, to David Parkins for so delightfully capturing the spirit of the times in his illustrations, to Win Fox (née Parker) who typed the manuscript, and to Doris Smith (née Allen), Paul Fox, John and Alison Phillips, Neville Richardson and Olive Riggall who made many helpful suggestions for inclusion.

Reg Woodward

104 Harrowby Road
Grantham

May 1984

I

I was born in the second month of 1919, on the eleventh day, an inauspicious beginning for someone who was to love cricket, hinting strongly that second eleven cricket and the last place in the batting order were to be my lot. My arrival must have served to throw into confusion a long established domestic order, since my parents had married over fifteen years earlier, and I was their first and only child. The house on Nettleham Road had been built for them on their marriage and was a commodious affair of five bedrooms, one of which my father used to give lessons in singing, so that from my earliest hours I grew accustomed to the sound of music. A modest garden at the front, and a fair-sized one, edged with apple trees, at the back, with a view of the central tower of the Cathedral and the sound of its bells, afforded a delightful place for a little boy to take his first unsteady steps.

The house contained a large entrance hall, with several pictures, including a print of St. Bernard dogs rescuing someone who had collapsed in the snow on the pass, and three photographs of the first cat my parents had, named Tiddles. There was an oak hatstand, containing Dad's walking sticks, a table with a gong, and a frame into which Dad inserted the Cathedral music sheet for the week. On one side was the dining room, bay windowed, with heavy Edwardian furniture, oil paintings, sideboard, dinner wagon, and oak mantelpiece. On the other was the drawing room with a great overmantel, a few nice pieces of porcelain, lots of photos in frames, various cabinets containing more china, and my mother's Bechstein upright piano. A passageway led to the kitchen, a small gloomy room with an imposing dresser with blue and white dinner service. When I was small it had a Victorian range with an oven, which mother used for drying firewood, never, so far as I can remember, for cooking, and a little side-boiler for hot water. It had to be black-leaded, a fearsome task, and was replaced by a modern fireplace about 1930. Finally came the scullery with its stone sink. There was a large pantry, and an outside lavatory, and very large coalhouse. Of the five bedrooms, the largest and nicest, at the front, was hardly ever used. The customs of the time were that you always kept the best unused, except for visits by royalty and relations, and my mother faithfully adhered to them. China, cutlery, bed linen, and much more, were included in the custom. Doris Allen only remembers the best silver being used twice in the five years she spent with us as housemaid cum nanny.

My father was born in Gloucester in 1874, so he was nearly fifty years of age by the time my memories of him begin. He was a big man,

~ He was a big man,
nearly six feet in height ~

nearly six feet in height and weighing seventeen stone. Almost all his life he had been a professional singer. As a boy he sang in the choir of New College, Oxford, and was educated at its Choir School. For six years he was solo boy in the choir, taking part in many performances in Christ Church Cathedral and the Sheldonian Theatre. Dad used to tell me about his life there, and how he had to wash outside under a pump, even in winter. He had two favourite stories. One of the clergy gave a Christmas party, and to his dismay found a little choirboy in tears. "What's the matter, my boy?" "Please, sir, I can't eat any more." "Never mind, fill your pockets". "Please, sir, I can't they're full already". He probably

My father as a choirboy at New College Oxford about 1888.

deserved some sympathy. Food wasn't very good. On one occasion the Head Master's wife asked a boy why he hadn't eaten up his dinner. "It's all pipes and gristles, mum", was the reply. The other one featured a youth who for a bet, one day before practice, peed on the fire which was laid ready for lighting. When it warmed up, the atmosphere became quite

~ The atmosphere became quite dreadful ~

dreadful, the choirmaster was both bewildered and appalled, and the practice was finished with some difficulty. When Dad left school, he worked in the booking office of the Great Western Railway in Gloucester, and before long was a Sunday baritone in the Cathedral Choir. He came to Lincoln in 1898, and lodged in St. Giles Avenue, next to the Lindum cricket ground.

Dad's family were all musicians. His elder brother, Tom, who had also been at New College, was a versatile man, organist and choirmaster of various churches, who played the tuba in Bournemouth Symphony Orchestra under Sir Dan Godfrey, and in the military band. He was for a time conductor of the Municipal Choir. In 1923 he moved to London where he played at Lyons, Piccadilly, as accompanist to both Albert Sandler and Alfredo Campoli. His younger brother Joseph, who died when only 39, stayed in Gloucester. Conductor of the Gloucester Instrumental Society, he played the violin in the Cheltenham Opera House Orchestra, and also conducted the Amateur Operatic Society. He was an able performer on piano, organ, violin, viola and cello, and a gifted teacher of music. Two of my father's cousins were also professional musicians. Will Woodward was for many years in the choir of Magdalen College, Oxford, and Joseph Wesley Woodward was a cellist in various orchestras at Eastbourne, where there is a monument to him on the seafront, since he was a member of the ship's orchestra which went down in the Titanic in 1912.

Grandfather Thomas Woodward was a musician, too. A native of West Bromwich, he was in his youth a holloware moulder and probably learnt his musicianship in Hilltop Methodist Chapel. He was born in Harvill's Hawthorn in 1841, married in Trinity Church in 1866, appears to have had a short spell in York Minster before coming to Gloucester in 1871, where he continued as bass lay clerk till his death in 1907. He kept a pony and trap, worked as a piano tuner, and also gave singing lessons. My grandmother Eliza, who died five months before him, was a Stackhouse from neighbouring Pelsall. Dad never talked much about his childhood, but that was probably because he left home when a very little lad, for Oxford. My uncle Tom's two daughters, however, had memories of the house in Brook Street as a very happy place, filled with kindness and laughter, with my father full of fun and jokes.

Dad still kept in touch with a delightful old lady who had been the maid in Brook Street when he was a lad. She was, by courtesy, Auntie Jennie, and I stayed for a week with her in Gloucester when I was about ten. She also spent a week with us and I fear Dad teased her unmercifully. "Have you heard the one about....." he would begin innocently. "Charlie, Charlie, not in front of the boy", expostulated Jennie, blushing a vivid scarlet. "Oh, it's quite alright", said Dad, "there was this...." "No, no, Charlie!" and he would keep this up for three or four minutes with great skill. Of course, there wasn't even a story to tell but he couldn't resist his bit of fun, and no doubt Jennie felt satisfied at the end of it, having successfully protected my innocence.

I have been able to trace the Woodwards back as far as 1600. In the early days they were nailors, and it is likely they were as miserably poor as all those who practised this trade, at which the whole family had to take a hand in order to survive. Cast iron holloware was first made in England in 1780, and it must have been from soon after that that family fortunes began to look up. My great grandfather Joseph, who died at 27, Hawkes Lane, West Bromwich in 1881, had risen to be manager of Hill Top Ironworks, and left £1,637.10.11, a considerable sum in those days.

But to come back to Dad. He was, as I said, a big man, which was not surprising, since he ate four good meals a day. A cooked breakfast, a substantial lunch, a hearty tea when he came in from Evensong at five o'clock, and a substantial supper at nine when he had finished giving singing lessons. He didn't seem to suffer from indigestion, went to bed at ten and rose at seven-thirty. Like many singers he enjoyed a glass, or two, or three, of beer, and smoked a pipe. He had a nap every day after lunch, and went everywhere on his broad feet, which he turned outwards at a considerable angle. They must have taken quite a lot of punishment and he visited a chiropodist regularly for attention to his corns. He always carried a walking stick and never went out without a hat. Both my parents made scathing remarks about 'the hatless brigade'. Most of the time he wore a presentable trilby, occasionally a cloth cap or a bowler. In summer he would don a straw boater which was a comic sight on such a big man. He had been blind in his left eye since his early twenties, but few people guessed it and it caused him no problems. He was helpless in domestic matters, unwilling and incapable of getting a simple meal. If anything had to be done, we sent for 'the man'. This was quite common in people of his generation, who took it for granted that maidservants, handymen, and gardeners would do whatever was needed. He did mow the lawn, but was liable to do more harm than good in the flower beds. From time to time he got a gardener to do a day or two's work, and once I was old enough I pruned the fruit trees which kept us supplied during the winter. Occasionally he would insist on drying the dishes. My mother, who feared breakages, tried to put him off. Dad insisted, but before long one or two plates and some cutlery would somehow slip from his fingers and land with a fearful crash on the scullery table. He never, in fact, broke anything, he was careful not to. Mum never saw through it.

On Wednesdays he went over to Gainsborough by train and gave singing lessons all day above a music shop, and in the spring conducted the amateur operatic society's annual week. He used to take me to see the matinee, and I remember 'Patience', 'the Gondoliers' and, my favourite, 'Les Cloches de Corneville'. On the second occasion he was anxious to show off his little son to the admiring ladies of the chorus and spent some time teaching me a song from 'the Gondoliers'. He took me into the dressing room, stood me on a cupboard and told me the ladies wanted me to sing it. I was frightened to death of all these painted women and it was with extreme difficulty that feeble piping sounds eventually emerged. I was well rewarded, though, a box of chocolates, and a kiss from every member of the chorus. I was very proud of my lipstick-covered face, and refused to have it washed until the performance was over! One Thursday morning he told my mother that he had broken his stick on the ladies of the chorus. I had wild visions of Dad pursuing them round the stage, lustily thwacking away. Well, how was I to know that his irritated banging on the music stand to correct their mistakes was too much for his baton?

We did not have too much in common. I think Dad found a small son rather wearing, and a big son worse still. However, we did play draughts amicably in the winter, and he would sometimes play cricket with me on the lawn. I imagine he had been a reasonable games player when young. He told me he had played cricket for the Lindum when he first came to Lincoln, and said that he could swim but hadn't done so for years. When I was old enough I used to accompany some of his best pupils on the piano and perhaps that was when we were closest. He was a fine musician and a gifted teacher, and I marvelled at his skills in producing remarkable results from people who were not particularly talented, and the wonderful range of expression in his own singing. It was a moving experience to hear him sing 'It is enough' from Mendelssohn's Elijah, or Schubert's 'Erlking'. He was equally at home though, with 'In Summertime on Bredon', or an audience-pleasing comic song, such as 'A Dinder Courtship'. If he had only been interested in German lieder, he would have been a marvellous exponent of the great Schubert and Schumann song cycles, and the works of Hugo Wolf and Brahms.

Dad had no hobbies, and when in 1935 he was told that his services in the Cathedral Choir would no longer be required, it nearly killed him. Even now, I can't understand the decision, he could have gone on singing for quite a few years, he was a superb musician, and his voice was still good. It was a cruel thing to do, his pride was terribly hurt, and he had no idea of what to do with his time. I was very distressed for him, and there was nothing we could do to soften the blow. There was worse to come. The miserable £1 a week pension the Cathedral gave to retired lay clerks did not materialise for the very good reason Dad had compounded it several years before to pay gambling debts to a bookmaker. This was no isolated affair, unhappily, since he was an addict, and several times my mother had used all her savings to keep him out of trouble. He couldn't get a job and we survived through the rents of some property my grandmother had left my mother. All through his married life, Dad was a victim of what can only be considered a disease. There were periodically terrible rows followed by periods when my mother refused to speak to him at all for a week or ten days. I dreaded these eruptions and they made me acutely unhappy. It is terrible to realise how one weakness can wreck a man's life. Dad was a gifted man musically, well-mannered, with a good sense of humour, kind in his dealings with people, very fond of animals, but all this was spoilt by his addiction to horse-racing. It led him into borrowing money from all sorts of people, until he reached a point where he could borrow no more. I was terribly hurt to find out when I was seventeen, that he borrowed money saying it was to pay for my education, for which in fact he never paid a penny. It's all nearly fifty years ago now, but I still find it very sad. It did have the result of making me very sympathetic in my teaching career to lads who had to cope with troubles at home.

My mother was born on January 29th, 1880 at 9, St. Mark's Street, Gloucester. She was educated privately at Bishop's Cleeve, Cheltenham and at Westfield House, Gloucester. She loathed the first establishment but was very happy at Westfield House. I have a pleasant picture of it, showing a handsome house, croquet on the lawn, a conservatory and some elegantly dressed young ladies. A prospectus of the time announces that the regular course of instruction comprises English language and literature, modern history and geography, French, German and Italian, Latin, Greek and ancient history, Scripture history, Arithmetic,

My mother in her wedding dress 1903.

Mathematics, Science, Piano, Harmonium, Singing, Theory of Music and Harmony, Drawing, geometrical, model and from the flat, Landscape and flower painting in oil and water-colours, plain and fancy needlework, dancing, callisthenics and drilling. Fees for boarders were twelve guineas per term for under tens, rising to twenty guineas for over

—My mother—

fifteens. My mother's interests were not academic, though spelling and arithmetic presented no problems. Map-making, drawing, needlework (she was exceptionally skilled in crocheting), and above all, music and dancing were her real interests. When she left school she worked with Miss Woodward (no relation) who ran a large dancing academy in Royal Crescent, Cheltenham, for whom she played the piano. When she married my father, she accompanied his pupils when they were being taught to sing difficult works. She continued her interest in ballroom dancing till she was over fifty years of age.

Her family was from the north of Worcester on her father's side and from Devon on her mother's. Her father was born at Martin Hussingtree in 1851. He was in the employment of Lord Bruton, probably as a groom and it is likely that that is how he met his future wife. Later he was employed by William Hicks, J.P. of Greville House, Kingsholm, Gloucester as a coachman. In later years he was the landlord of the Railway Hotel (now St. James), St. James Place, Cheltenham in two spells 1889-1899, and 1906-07. When he retired he moved across the road to 12, Ambrose Street. He and his wife worked very hard at the Hotel, which is probably why my mother was a boarder at school. They had little leisure, but when, occasionally, he could take three days off, he would go off in his pony and trap wherever it took his fancy. They could never be away together. Gran's idea of a good time was to take the train to Weston-Super-Mare, then the boat to Ilfracombe. One thing was for

My grandmother about 1875.

sure. No matter how many people were ill in rough weather, Gran wouldn't be.

Thomas Huphnill, his father, born at Martin Hussingtree, just north of Worcester, was a labourer who became a shepherd at Lady Wood. The census of 1861 mentions his eldest son, Thomas, who at the age of fifteen was working as a carter's boy for William Hall, a farmer with 200 acres, employing six labourers, two boys, plus four women, an interesting light on the large numbers needed on a farm in the mid nineteenth century. It would have been a hard life, exposed to every kind of weather, inadequately fed and clothed. I was only two when grandad died, so I can't really remember him.

My grandmother, however, lived with us from about 1924 till her death in 1930. Even in old age she was a strikingly handsome woman. Born in Langford Budville on the edge of the Quantocks in Somerset in 1845, she was lady's maid at Hestercombe House before her marriage. Her father was a native of Tiverton, a cordwainer when a young man, who moved to Somerset and became a millwright. The Radfords were yeoman farmers in Sandford near Crediton as early as 1700. We had something of a love/hate relationship. She read to me by the hour, taught me to read and write, and to do sums. She loved playing games, cards, ludo, snakes and ladders, anything that came to hand. Unfortunately she used to tease me unbearably when I lost, and when I could stand it no longer and got in my belated retaliation, she would complain to my mother and drop hints about my upbringing. The house revolved around her to a considerable extent and she must have been pretty demanding. She had no great opinion of Dad, due to his gambling, but it must be said that he accepted her in the house for several years, and deserves credit for that. I only wish there had been tape recorders in the 1920's. She must have had a wealth of interesting memories. She wore magnificent high Victorian black dresses, with lace ruffles, an elaborate hairdo and a little pocket watch. She had a fine treadle sewing machine and proved very expert indeed with it, curtains, dresses, alterations, all came easy to her. I imagine this was due to her training as a lady's maid. If anything needed doing in this line, she did it, since my mother loathed sewing and hated using the machine.

My mother was small, weighed a mere eight stone, less than half what Dad weighed! But she was very strong-willed and the dominant power in the home. She knew virtually nothing about house-keeping when she married, but learnt quickly. We ate well, though often far too much of what was not good in quantity, potatoes, pastry, cakes, bread. All our pastry and cake was home-made, so was jam and marmalade, eggs were preserved for the winter. We had plenty of meat, and fish, always fried in batter. I'm not sure our gas stove even had a grill. Mother kept a book into which she copied all kinds of recipes, and made strenuous attempts to vary what we ate, a different pudding every day, different ways of using up the Sunday joint, different ways of serving

My father, about 1900.

My grandmother, about 1910.

eggs at breakfast. She kept a little penny note book in which she dutifully recorded every penny spent on house-keeping during the week. Periodically she looked through it to check the rise and fall of prices, which in the twenties were relatively stable. Fires meant a lot of work, and water for a bath was heated in the copper and carried upstairs in buckets. We only had gas lighting till about 1936, and I went to bed with a candle, quite dangerous, really, since I liked to read in bed. The gas light was not always turned up fully so as to 'save' – a magic word to my mother – which I didn't appreciate much, finding homework at times a strain on the eyes. The large house was kept beautifully clean, which was fine, but there was a great emphasis on tidiness, which was hard, since I had no room of my own for homework and hobbies, and I seemed to be always having to clear up and put things away so that the table could be laid for meals. I used the table for toy soldiers, homemade cricket and football games, drawing and model making. I made stations, signal boxes and lots more for my model railway, and then became interested in the theatre, making a model theatre and designing sets for the Shakespeare plays I knew.

Mother was inclined to be shy with strangers. We entertained very little, and when we did it was always for tea, best china, potted meat, tinned peaches, wafers of bread and butter, homemade cake and pastry. The cakes Mum made for Christmas and my birthday were superb and I've never met better. After Gran died we couldn't afford a maid, and just had a women in once a week to do rough work. Mum did all the shopping and every day she went down hill, where food was marginally cheaper than in the Bail, and trudged up Steep Hill with a heavy basketful. She learnt to knit, mainly socks, but had little recreation. She liked reading and the Public Library provided her with a regular diet of Ethel M. Dell, Annie Swan, Muriel Hine, Ruby Ayres and the rest of the sisterhood. When I was small she escorted me to the pictures and quite enjoyed it, but would never go on her own. The problems and uncertainty caused by Dad's gambling gradually soured her, and she had a lot to put up with. We all think at times of how things might have been different, but it doesn't do us much good, I fear.

Both my parents gave me much love and care, but there are problems in being an only child of elderly parents. Since I was all they were likely to have, they were over-protective both as regards my health and my companions. I could never bring a friend home without asking first, and although permission was usually given, it was often hedged around. My conduct, too, was always considered in the light of its bearing upon what people would think of the way I was brought up, and could be niggling! I liked an open-necked shirt in hot weather, but that was letting the side down lamentably. No doubt my indignant "why" and "why not?" were a sore trial to them, but there did seem to a little boy a lot of desirable things that could not be done. There was, for instance, a total block on the possession of a bicycle. In fact I never had one while I was at school, it was held to be too dangerous. My friends all had one, and I was the odd man out.

Nevertheless, I had a happy childhood, was well fed and clothed, had a holiday each year, and even if I had little in the way of possessions, I had such a busy life once I joined the choir, that it didn't matter very much. From then on, I began to go my own way, realising even as a small boy, that I hadn't that much common ground with my parents. We just weren't interested in the same things. In my latter years at school, I discussed my future with the staff, and made my own decisions. My parents were quite willing for me to stay on at school, and put no pressure on me to leave and get a job, and that was a big thing in those days. I have much for which to be thankful to them.

II

In the week of my birth, Dean Fry spoke in Convocation about Evolution, Adam and Eve and the Flood, to be violently attacked by the Revd. MacTurk, vicar of Holland Fen, for his advanced views. The vicar had been a chorister in the Cathedral under Young, Bennett's predecessor and was a British Israelite! In the city itself, Ruston and Hornsby were discussing amalgamation with Ransomes of Ipswich, and Lincoln City F.C., having just beaten their old rivals Grimsby Town, managed to lose 1-0 to Bradford City who thus brought to an end a run of ten successive defeats! The Theatre Royal was staging a play entitled 'The man who stayed at home', the Palace Theatre (later the Plaza cinema) had a comedy revue called 'Fragments', the Picture House (later the Regal) was showing (Monday to Wednesday) a serial 'Vengeance and the Woman', and 'A Spinner of Dreams', followed (Thursday to Saturday) by 'Tilly's punctured romance' and 'Highway of Hope'.

Later that year, in June, Mr. T. R. Coombes resigned the Headship of the Choir School to move to Llandaff and in August the Lincoln Firm, Ruston and Hornsby, produced a five seater tourer. I can remember seeing some of them when I became old enough to recognise cars.

I remember little of my earlier years, except that we had a maid called Elsie, and a cat called Monchy after a village in France to which a pre-war lodger, an engineering student at Ruston's, called Reginald Barnard-Smith, was posted in 1916. My mother liked the name, my father thought I should bear his name and my maternal grandmother felt that her daughter's maiden name should be preserved, so I ended up Reginald Charles Huphnill Woodward when on Palm Sunday I entered Lincoln Cathedral for the first time and was duly baptised in the ancient font in the nave by the Precentor, Canon Wakeford. When I in due course reached the Prep at Lincoln School, these names caused me considerable embarrassment, and I found it expedient to suppress the third altogether. My contemporaries poked fun at the Reginald, and I wished my parents had chosen something unremarkable, such as John.

The doctor who brought me into the world was Doctor Darbyshire and he attended us until I was about sixteen. He had his medicines made up at his house and many is the bottle of iron tonic and the like that I swallowed at his behest. I would advise no child to allow himself to be considered delicate. There are so many nasty things to be taken. Cod

~ There are so many nasty things to be taken ~

liver oil was to me unspeakably vile, for instance. Great importance was attached to being regular, and the most loathsome remedy for this was senna pods, guaranteed to produce immediate and unpleasant results, even worse than brimstone and treacle.

In those days my father gave lessons in singing to as many as fifty pupils a week, so the house was very busy, especially on Fridays, market day in Lincoln, when country pupils arrived and departed throughout the day. Each day had its own order and pattern of housework, and seasonal variations of winter and summer curtains, and spring and autumn cleaning came and went, paintwork all washed, carpets doused with tea leaves and salt to bring out the colour. I hated spring cleaning. I couldn't

Doris about 1928.

go anywhere without getting into trouble. "Don't go in there, I've just cleaned it and you'll make it dirty", my mother would bellow in a ladylike way.

When I was four years old my mother took a wise decision and engaged a young girl of fifteen as a housemaid/nanny. Doris was a Derbyshire lass from Alfreton and had a little brother about my age, and my life was transformed. Endlessly kind and inventive, she took me out in the pram each afternoon, devised all kinds of games for the garden, read to me when the weather was bad and patiently answered all my questions. When she arrived in August, 1923, it was for a wage of ten shillings per month, living in, one month's holiday in August, two weeks at Christmas. On duty, such as answering the door, she wore a white apron and a little white cap. She was allowed to go out on Thursday evenings, when she usually went to a dance at the Conservative Club, but had to be in by nine, and she was able to go out to tea on one Sunday in the month. Every tea-time the daily paper, the Daily Express, was ceremonially handed over for her to read.

The mornings were given over to housework and the preparation of meals. A great deal of very hard work was needed to run a house in the 1920's, beginning on Monday morning with washday. Water was boiled

~ Beginning on Monday morning with washday ~

in a gas copper, then ladled into an enormous wooden washing machine, which was cranked by turning a handle on a large wheel, no easy matter when soaking material was being agitated in the water. Most of the moisture was removed by means of a large mangle with wooden rollers. Clothes were boiled in the copper, rinsed in the sink, blued (to make them white!), starched, folded, mangled and put out to dry in the garden. On a good drying day, they could be brought in dry, damped, folded, mangled and ironed. The irons were heated on the black-leaded kitchen range, and sticks for firelighting were dried in its sideoven. Lastly, the table top, the pantry, and the scullery floor were all scrubbed.

I didn't like Mondays, and soon learnt to make myself inconspicuous. Too many unpredictable things could go wrong, with all too predictable effects on my mother's temper. No sooner was everything pegged out on the line, than it all had to be brought in because it had started to rain. Or articles leapt off the line onto the grass, got dirty and had to be done all over again.

Coal fires meant a lot of work and my mother's aversions to any artificial aids such as fire lighters and gas pokers, meant that frequently they gave trouble and disproved the saying that there is no smoke without fire. The kitchen range was blackleaded once a week, there seemed to be brassware in need of regular polish everywhere, and hands were constantly in water for cleaning and preparing food.

Wednesdays were a popular day with me, since that was the only day Doris was allowed to take me down town, being the day that all the shops were shut. My weekly treat was for the pram to be stationed by the G.N. level crossing in High Street so that I could see the exciting, steam-belching, engines at marvellously close quarters. Needless to say, I had decided what my future career was to be.

Fridays were baking day for cakes and pastry. I preferred pastry to cake, especially the eccles cakes my mother made every week, and the little lemon curd tarts which Dad referred to as Vaseline tarts. Every week my mother took a small offering of pastry to two old ladies in the cottages across the road, and in course of time this task was often entrusted to me.

Each afternoon Doris took me out in the pram, while my parents had forty, or more, winks. I had a weak ankle, which was supposed to need strengthening by walking, and Doris had strict instructions to make me do just that. Loud cries of woe greeted the dreaded moment, but orders were orders, though at times Doris joined the ranks of the unloved. In those days the town ended within about a mile of our house, the shortest distance to the country being our own road where houses ended at the Nightingale. There was Greetwell Road with the prison, and sometimes gangs of prisoners working outside, and further on, the ironstone mines with little underground workings and small-gauge railway line. Most beautiful of all was Burton Road with the fine avenue of trees after the new (now the Sabraon) barracks and occasionally we would come upon a marching column, led, if we were lucky, by a band. The totally unexpected can be frightening to a small child, and once on Greetwell Road, hordes of teenagers in strange dress erupted from the woods and dashed across the road, temporarily surrounding us. It was, however, merely senior boys from the Grammar School, in football kit, on a cross country run.

I spent golden hours in the garden. Doris made me a bow and arrow from a garden cane, an Indian head-dress with real feathers, a crowning glory to the blanket draped around my shoulders and a tent was constructed out of beansticks and an old sheet. A large weeping willow could

~ I spent golden hours in the garden ~

represent the Amazon jungle, or a Robinson Crusoe type hut after shipwreck on a desert island, the boat being a large wooden box on a wooden roller, which rocked most convincingly as we paddled frantically to escape the fury of the pounding surf. But Doris' priceless gift was to teach me to play cricket. As befitted a native of a major cricketing county, she was greatly my superior in both batting and bowling, though, come to think of it, that seems to have been true of most of those with whom I have since played. Over fifty years later, to my delight, she was able to come as my guest to the annual dinner of the Lincolnshire County Cricket Club in my year as President.

Doris was a Congregationalist, but usually worshipped in Rasen Lane Methodist Church close at hand. Sometimes she took me with her. She tells me my favourite hymn was 'Hushed was the evening hymn", but honesty compels me to admit that I really can't remember. Occasionally as she returned home she would see my father emerging from the Turk's Head. "Ah, Doris, now, not a word to Mrs. Woodward", the exhortation being accompanied by half-a-crown.

In the winter we played table games, Ludo, Snakes and Ladders, and various card games, in all of which my grandmother took an enthusiastic part. Most exciting of all was a Christmas Concert, attended by elderly ladies from the cottages across the road. Recitations, songs and plays were assiduously learnt, a curtain was strung up across the kitchen and a riotous half hour began. We appeared in a variety of costumes and parts, to tumultuous applause from our captive audience. I was affected little by stage fright, but suffered from a tendency to hysterical giggling at inauspicious moments. A pirate chief unable to order someone to walk the plank because he can't stop laughing, is at a considerable disadvantage.

My second lot of teeth caused me terrible trouble, since they were too many for my mouth. I suffered untold misery at the hands of an incompetent dentist who, instead of removing enough of them, made me wear a fearful contraption which pulled and pushed in various directions and caused me months of pain. It didn't do any good, and the problem was not resolved till a cricket ball removed the tooth that was surplus to requirement, when I was keeping wicket.

A weekly treat was a visit to the cinema. My first visit must have been when I was five or six. My Aunt Nellie, actually my mother's cousin, took me to a cinema in Gloucester, thinking I would enjoy Charlie Chaplin. All went well till poor Charlie got his feet stuck in some tar and couldn't move. I was appalled by the callous attitude of the audience who actually laughed at his predicament. I foresaw a tragic end, howled the place down, and was led out, inconsolable. However, I got over it in time, and on Wednesday afternoons was to be found at the Grand at the top of High Street, the Picture House, later called the Regal, or the Corn Exchange. The cinema was flourishing and soon the Central, with beautifully painted murals, and the Plaza, were in operation. Cowboy films were my favourite, and in those early days my mother, who loathed them, must have seen thousands of Indians bite the dust. Pirates weren't bad either, but I didn't like precious time wasted by the hero and heroine going into a lengthy clinch. Until I learned to read, I needed an interpreter for the words flashed on the silent screen. The only sounds were those of the indefatigable pianist, pounding away music appropriate to the epic deeds enacted in front of my fascinated eyes. Seats were sixpence, ninepence and one shilling. Sixpence meant a likelihood of fleas, so that was out, a shilling was too much, so ninepence it was. A performance was on the principle of two houses a night, matinees Wednesday and Saturday. Later on, the so called continuous performance came into being. As well as a feature film, there would be British Movietone News, possibly Pathetone Pictorial, and probably a short slapstick comedy. The Central went in for serials, each episode ending with Doctor Fu-manchu dropping the hero into the snakepit, tying him on the rails just before the coming express, or whatever.

The talkies arrived in Lincoln about 1932; films in colour somewhat later. Most were to be in black and white till well after the war. In the mid thirties the Odeon was built, with a prestigious organ, followed soon after by the Ritz. There was no cinema uphill till 1937, when the Radion was built. They all had their characteristics. The Corn Exchange lacked a sloping auditorium, and was bad for seeing, the Picture House had a cafe attached, the Central had exotic murals, palm-fringed beaches, deserts, Moorish palaces, etc., the Plaza had been a music hall, the Grand was small, narrow and friendly. In the intervals, spotlights picked out the more glamorous attendants, who came round selling ice-cream. I never ceased to take delight in the adventures of Charlie Chaplin, Harold Lloyd, and Buster Keaton, gradually outgrew cowboys and indians, acquired a taste for historical romances such as the Prisoner of Zenda, the Three Musketeers, and never greatly cared for musicals or the Marx brothers. I can't remember individual films very well, but Metropolis, All Quiet on the Western Front, and Ben Hur were memorable.

We had no radio in the house, my mother refused to have one till after I had passed my A. Levels. This did not worry me greatly, though on occasion I would have enjoyed it, and since I have always liked absolute quiet when working, its absence was more blessing than curse.

I must have been about five when Dad brought home a comic, with the adventures of Tiger Tim in glorious technicolour. I was enthralled, agitated vociferously for more and was successful. At the age of about nine I moved over to 'The Adventure' and occasionally 'The Rover' and 'The Wizard'. I can only remember the title of one story, Morgan the Mighty. Often something or other was given away with an edition, metal battleships of the Royal Navy, for instance, and I can remember a little book in which, in 1928, I gummed, week by week, the Australian touring party. When I was about twelve I became hooked on the Magnet, Greyfriars, Billy Bunter and Mr. Quelch afforded me endless delight, and since I swapped them with Tommy Kirkby for copies of the Gem, I was able to enjoy that, too. We then found that there were little monthly booklets and managed to get those, as well. From September onwards a brisk campaign was mounted to secure the Christmas Annual.

Books were another matter. Once I learnt to read, my appetite knew no bounds, and books were treasured possessions. The Coral Island started me off on Ballantyne and I devoured Henty. School stories were different. I liked Tom Brown's Schooldays, but was bewildered by Eric or Little by Little. The school stories of the day had certain standard features. Games figured prominently, the little hero thrashed a big bully, the baddies smoked, cribbed and sneaked into pubs, and sometimes even stole money, lessons seemed to consist of Latin and little else. Could school really be like this? It didn't seem very attractive, especially the beatings, detentions and impositions. My godfather lent me some bound copies of the Strand Magazine and with the discovery of Sherlock Holmes my reading life took on a new direction and dimension.

My parents were not too keen on the Public Library books because 'you never know where they have been or what you might pick up'. There may well have been some truth in this because some of the popular books were distinctly grubby and smelt disagreeable. My mother insisted on their being covered with paper before I read them. The Public Library shelves were full of stories by Agatha Christie, Freeman Wills Crofts, Dorothy Sayers, G. K. Chesterton and all my other favourites. There was, however, a monumental snag. In the eyes of the Library authorities I was far too young at eleven years old to be allowed to borrow books from the adult section. I was not prepared to wait for years. I had the initiative to bring home an application form for dad and get him to join. I appropriated his ticket and from then on, little liar that I was, explained that I was fetching books for my father. By the age of twelve I could read two hundred books a year quite happily, but unfortunately this coincided with an unprofitable period in my studies and my reading was often threatened with parental interdict. There were also, by the mid-thirties, lending libraries in the town, twopence per week being the usual charge, and I became a patron of the Chain Library. I would have liked to belong to Boots, where a class A subscription entitled you to the newest books, but that was far beyond my straitened circumstances. My love of reading is associated with a painful memory of my adolescent years. I was fourteen at the time, and that Christmas a parcel arrived from Auntie Clarry. Oh, great, obviously a book! Knowing how scatty she was, I should have been warned. I unwrapped it in haste. Fairy Tales of old Tyrol. I have seldom been so insulted and mortified.

III

The Lincoln of my childhood was a good place to grow up in. Nettleham Road was quite different from what it is today. The old road was narrow and where the northern carriageway is now, the trees on the island being inside a fine old stone wall, which, as it left Northgate, bent round to the right to the picturesque row of cottages long since demolished. There was little traffic when I was small, a horse and van delivered our bread, a horse and open trap our milk, neither of which would have satisfied today's health requirements. The milk was just taken out of the churn by a dipper and transferred to a jug at our back door. It came from a tiny farm on Eastgate which backed on to the cemetery behind St. Giles Avenue, kept by people named Wright. A few people trundled by on bicycles, old men appeared with barrows and shovels to collect the horse dung for their allotments. Buses appeared for the first time in 1928. All around us the properties had fine trees, as did many of the roads uphill, the far end of Burton Road and Greetwell Road being particularly splendid. Just down the grove was the Lindum Cricket Ground where I spent many happy hours. Minster Yard and Steep Hill have changed little. Bailgate meant Mr. Payne's grocer's shop, full of interesting smells which could be tracked down, and the bonus of occasionally being invited to help myself to a free biscuit from one of the tins on the counter. Mr. Brummitt's greengrocery, the rival pork

Northgate about 1930 before the road was widened with Dad on his way to the Cathedral.

butchers, Inkley and Curtis, Mr. Leachman's butcher's shop, all were familiar ports of call. My mother bought lots of little things from Miss Hill's shop near Newport Arch, and then the way home led past the miniature fire station and the row of cottages in Church Lane where I was friends with a white whiskered old man named Darby.

As I grew older, I explored the many interesting corners of the city, Vicars' Court, James Street, Brayford Pool, Greestone Stairs, the Arboretum which then boasted fountains and a conservatory, the little stepped streets in the vicinity of Spring Hill and much else. Trams ran to the Stonebow end of High Street and it was quite an adventure to go down to Bracebridge. When buses first came up Lindum Hill, my father feared the worst, but when none of them got out of control and crashed with great loss of life, he accepted and eventually used them. They had to be single deckers because incredibly they squeezed through Pottergate Arch at the bottom end of Minster Yard on the downhill run. The great estates at the north end of the city were built during my childhood. The village of Nettleham was reached by a country walk, since there were no houses beyond the Nightingale Inn and one mile further on was the Roaring Meg, a comic name for a tiny stream barely a foot wide. Downhill was industry and shops. There were the prestige establishments such as Mawer and Collingham's, the many family concerns, Boots, which had a lift – the snooty attendant was inclined to tell children to walk upstairs – Ruddock's, which as a bookshop came high on my list, the various cinemas, the public library, and when I was older, Sincil Bank, the home of Lincoln City Football Club.

The Arboretum was the scene of band concerts every Sunday evening in the summer. All the works had their own brass band, with an

~ It had a large statue of a lion ~

The picturesque row of cottages opposite our house. Note the delightful tower cottage in the centre.

annual competition in the Drill Hall. On Whit Monday great numbers of children gathered for the annual Sunday School treat. It had a very large statue of a lion, which on more than one occasion became a tiger overnight, having suffered the indignity of being painted in unbecoming stripes by vandals. There was an ornamental pond, and, most exciting of all, a waterfall, all of three feet in height!

The Fair was held in Spring on the cattle market on Monks Road. To a child it was a fairyland of colour, light, excitement, strange smells of hot steam engines, and deafening sounds of cheerfully competing steam organs. I was taken at a quite early age, under convoy. Doris enjoyed it, too, and abided faithfully by the prohibitions attached to any roundabout which might be dangerous. Thus, steamboats, the cakewalk and flying chairs were out. However, the various roundabouts were so enjoyable that I didn't mind too much. Sometimes Dad was given a coconut which had been won by someone he knew and I drank the milk with great pleasure. In between rides, I gazed, fascinated, at the mechanical figures of the steam organs as they banged their drums and cymbals. Sideshows of bearded women, fattest man in the world, and the like, did not interest me, and neither did games of chance for prizes. But the enormous steam engines were well worth some moments of study, and there was the mysterious world of the caravans in which the showmen lived.

Sometimes our perambulations took in Wickham Gardens under the shadow of the great water tower. There were tennis courts, a bowling green and an open-air swimming bath, and one of the First World War tanks which had been made in Lincoln and was placed there as a sort of monument. Tanks were invented by Sir William Tritton and first made in Lincoln. To keep the thing secret, the workers were told that these strange things were tanks for water for use in Mespotamia, and that is how they got their name.

Neither of my parents liked dogs. We nearly always had a canary in which I wasn't very interested, then when I was about nine we acquired a cat, a gorgeous blue Persian we named Pompey. He was playful, affectionate and really beautiful, and we spent hours together. Like all long-haired cats, his fur easily got clots and much grooming was needed, which he bore with good humour. Indoors he had riotous games with a pingpong ball, which he never managed to kill, and enjoyed a rabbit's foot dragged along on a piece of string. In the winter he sat on my lap, purring noisily and companionably. His interest in what was going on was not always welcome when I had hobbies or homework on the table, since he didn't in the least mind sitting on the exercise book I urgently needed. He killed birds very occasionally, which brought down my mother's wrath upon him, but there were few mice about and no rats, so he was normally unable to lay such offerings proudly at my feet. I loved him dearly and was heartbroken when he was killed by a car when he was six years old. Animals give us so much in return for so little, and greatly

~ a gorgeous blue Persian we named Pompey ~

enrich our lives. He was as beautiful in nature as he was in appearance.

Christmas was celebrated in some style. The dining room was decorated with paper streamers, an artificial Christmas tree was hung with glittering ornaments and a few halfpenny bars of chocolate or sweets. It also had little candles which Dad used to light on Christmas evening with magical effect, while we roasted chestnuts in the grate. It was a time of formidable eating. My mother used to boil and press a tongue, which, together with a ham, replaced the usual breakfast fare. A large pork pie was also in attendance. Lunch was the traditional turkey, followed by home-made Christmas pudding. Mother always made at least two, one being saved for my birthday early in February. If there was any room left, there were mincepies, also home-made. Tea featured a home-made Christmas cake, covered in marzipan paste and icing, decorated with sweets and little figures. I was not allowed to see and unwrap my presents till after breakfast. Moments of deep satisfaction and disappointment were mingled. Like all children I didn't find it easy to appear grateful for something I didn't really want. Dates, figs and chocolates, orange and lemon slices were doled out during the evening, and the digestive juices really worked flat out. My mother could be made very happy by the gift of a jar of ginger. For Dad, Christmas was about the only time he smoked a cigar rather than his pipe. For a few days before Christmas carol singers would come round. Some of them sang quite well and even met with Dad's approval. When I became older I discovered a nasty feature of Christmas, being made to write 'thank you' letters. 'What shall I say'? was my unhappy theme song, as I sat in misery before a writing pad and a pile of envelopes.

Shrove Tuesday was marked by pancakes, always eaten with lemon juice and sugar. They were so good I thought it was silly to confine them to that day, but my propaganda had little effect. On Good Friday we had hot-cross buns for breakfast, but these didn't excite me.

"What shall I say?"

A great treat was a visit to the Castle, a much more exciting place than it is today. The turret was reached by a difficult little wooden stair, replaced many years ago, and there was spread out a panorama of the whole city, and a stunning view of the Cathedral West Front over a lovely collection of red roofs. In those days it was possible to see most of the old prison, the gloomy cells with their great iron doors, the exercise yards, and the chapel, so arranged that every prisoner could see the Chaplain but not one of his fellow prisoners. In the great keep could be seen the graves of prisoners who had died in prison and been buried there, tiny tombstones with just initials and a date. It was reached by climbing a long and very steep stairway, a frightening prospect when descending, since there was no rail, and the steps are very, very steep and worn.

One of my father's pupils was Hilda Baldock, whose husband was killed in the War soon after they were married. She lived with her parents, two unmarried sisters, Gladys, an enormous young woman who worked in the bakehouse, Edith, a schoolteacher, and an unmarried brother, Arnold. They were the village bakers and kept a general store, as well. It was considered that country air would benefit me, and she kindly invited me to Misterton, near Gainsborough, where they lived. They were delightful, kind people and I loved every moment of it. There was the bakehouse, the lovely smell of fresh bread, the odd tart that came my way, the walks through the fields, with nobody minding if my shoes got dirty (a terrible sin at home) and a marvellously happy atmosphere. They were Methodists and took me to Chapel and Sunday School, which seemed very strange after worship in the Cathedral. I still remember the fields of daffodils, the lock gates of the little canal and the great procession of fancy dress through the village on what I imagine must have been Whit Monday.

IV

When I first watched cricket on the Lindum, the pitch ran east and west, but that was changed within a year. The rugby pitch of today exists on top of the remains of a quarry, which was filled in in the early thirties, and a tram was used as a sort of grandstand by the sight screen at the Wragby Road end of the cricket ground. It is a fine ground with the Cathedral towers in the background. The old wooden pavilion was taken down when the present buildings were erected in 1969. Major Wilson arrived for games in a prestigious Rolls Royce with the battery on the running board, various people arrived in August, sporting caps of startling design and colour, and one or two members of the staff of Lincoln School played there, Mr. Marriott, Mr. Phillips and Mr. Dollery. Before long I became the operator of the old scoreboard, which gave me access to the pavilion enclosure and the possibility of studying my heroes at close quarters. One of the worst deprivations I suffered on joining the Cathedral Choir was having to miss a large part of each Saturday's game to sing Evensong. The cricket was very enjoyable, having the best of amateur cricket along with the worst. Every attempt was made to achieve a result, but it must be said that a 2.30 start often meant the teams did not take the field much before three o'clock. 6.30 was the usual finishing time and there was, of course, no cricket on Sunday.

It was on the Lindum that I first learned to love the game that has given me so much pleasure. It must be now nearly sixty years ago that my father, little realising the consequences of his action, asked me if I would like to go with him to watch the cricket. I wasn't over keen but ever dutiful I went. I have never ceased to be glad I did so. My first hero was Major Cowley. He closely resembled Mr. Pickwick, but nonetheless excitement was at fever pitch when he batted. My recollection is that most of the time he hit the ball in the air, but almost always to

~ most of the time he hit the ball in the air ~

untenanted parts of the field. I don't think he was capable of running very much, which was terribly rough luck on the bowler who had to bowl to the end at which he had taken root. I have learnt since that when Lindum had to field he used to say, "Skipper, do you mind if I wear tennis shoes? Get about a bit better, you know". Since the only time he was ever known to move from slip was when the field changed ends, it shows he wasn't lacking a sense of humour. George Wright who used to hit the ball into adjacent gardens more often than not, Charles Wilson, Gervas Wells-Cole, Martin Shaw, Billy Rose, what cricketing characters for a small boy to gaze on in awe and admiration. My father used to have some rough Saturday mornings as I badgered him remorselessly as to whether all my favourites would be in the team that afternoon.

The gates of paradise having been ajar for some weeks, my father announced one day that they would be flung wide open. 'It's cricket week next week'. 'What's that, Dad?' I could not credit my good fortune. Cricket every day for a week, and in the morning, too. I remember little Mr. Barber, all 4'6" of him bowling his underhand tweakers for Sheffield Collegiate, and Mr. Blaxland of the Derbyshire Friars, one of the cleanest hitters it has ever been my good fortune to watch.

As far as my parents were concerned, only the lower orders went to football matches. I was even ignorant of the very existence of Lincoln

City until I was ten years old when they narrowly failed to gain promotion from the Third Division (North) to the Second Division. In 1932 they were successful and I avidly devoured their performances as chronicled in the Football Echo. Naturally I wanted to go and see them play. I had to work at it. So long as I was in the choir there was little chance, since only during the short holidays at Christmas and Easter was Saturday afternoon free. Finally I was despatched under escort of one of my friends and his father. I enjoyed it very much and once I left the choir I seldom missed a match. It may be the rosy haze of time, but I think football was more fun in those days, attackers took defenders on, skill wasn't stifled, and there were lots of players I enjoyed watching. The goalkeeper was a veteran, Dan McPhail, who had come from Portsmouth, there was a large and rugged defender named Jim Smith at left back, who did to others what we certainly did not wish them to do to our players, a left-half named George Whyte who scored countless goals from free kicks – it was before anyone had thought of a wall – a centre forward, Johnnie Campbell, who was studying to be a pharmacist, a right-half of considerable elegance, Alf Horne, who converted 32 out of 33 penalty kicks while he was with City; he only missed one and that was a day when City beat Barrow 6-0. Just before the war City had a delightful left-winger who later became a notable Test Match umpire. I wonder if Tom Spencer ever thinks of his year on City's books. One or two players on either side in those days might well have been seen labouring under the handicap of a beer belly. They didn't run about too much, but were often delightfully skilful. Crowds were usually in the region of 7,000 – 8,000, they were vociferous, but violence was unthinkable. Happy days, indeed!

I was eighteen before I saw First Division football, Roland Hayes' father taking us one Wednesday to see Derby County, who thrashed Wolves 5-0, and followed this up by demolishing Arsenal's famous defensive system by a similar score, Astley registering a hat-trick. At Notts. County I saw the diminutive Hughie Gallagher, well past his best, produce an unforgettable moment, when, with his back to the goal, he back heeled the ball unerringly into the corner of the net from twelve yards out. But Sincil Bank was home, a lovely green pitch, the engine drivers on the railway embankment halting for as long as they dared, to see what was happening, the excitement as the red and white striped shirts of our lads converged on the opposing goal, the discussions that ran on for two weeks till the next home game, the two mile walk uphill back home which restored circulation on freezingly cold days, the delight when a really good victory was secured, the misery of wasted opportunities, the interest of a new signing, and hope renewed with the coming of a new season.

I was keen to learn to play the piano, and at the age of nine I had my first teacher, Mr. Harry Trevitt, organist of St. Peter-in-Eastgate, and at one time Dr. Bennett's assistant at the Cathedral. A very small, dapper man, he managed to live to be over one hundred years old. He was a very competent musician and technically a good teacher, but suffered from a massive lack of understanding of little boys. Music should be enjoyable and fun, and tension is an enemy to be feared. His system was that you did not go on to a new piece until the present one was note perfect. The net result of all this was that I was so tense I inevitably made a mistake or two. After a year I wasn't enjoying it and had to be driven to practise. I then had a year of Miss Stockwell, who tried hard, the faults this time, I fear, being on my side. In my defence I must say that the demands of school, choir and homework didn't leave much free time and I grudged giving some of it to practice every day, especially in the summer. Lessons, therefore, ceased. I never, in fact, had any more from that time, but a genuine love of music brought me back to the piano after about a year, and I knew enough to teach myself. I played when I wanted to and had time, and loved it. Music has been very much a part of my life ever since and an abiding joy.

Relatively few families owned cars in those days, and as a small boy, Lincoln was to me the world. Every year I left it for two weeks, by bus if to a Lincolnshire seaside town, otherwise by train.

I loved trains. The varieties of engine and rolling stock, faithfully reproduced by Hornby, and greatly coveted as I gazed at them in toyshop windows, the amazing speeds on main lines – a mile a minute! – and the interest of watching a quite different landscape flash by the window, all those combined to make a train journey almost the best part of the holiday. The old fashioned carriages, not very comfortable always, the occasional corridor coaches, had one thing that never failed to delight me, the pictures behind the seats, of beauty spots served by the line. I inspected and evaluated, busily making plans and filing away information in preparation for an offensive aimed at the choice of the next year's holiday. The railway network was very extensive and delightful branch lines were everywhere, often giving lovely views unobtainable from the roads. Just once in my little life I travelled in a Pullman Car, from London to Brighton. What magical opulence! For those lucky enough to enjoy it, it could be a gracious age.

As a little lad I hardly ever travelled in a car. The first bus journey I can remember was from Lincoln to Wragby. A friend of my parents had a bus which did this journey – there were lots of small one man bus companies in the twenties. Vic's bus ignominiously broke down at Langworth, but was happily soon put to rights. While we were waiting, I was thirsty and was given a drink by a cottager from the water butt. It tasted a bit odd and my parents weren't pleased when I told them. I must have been about six at the time. When I went to stay in Misterton I could go out with Arnold when he delivered bread from the van, a great thrill, as he greeted all his customers and told me who they were. Cars were very interesting in those days because they were so markedly different. Lordly Rolls Royces, with the battery on the running board, baby Austins, Morgan threewheelers, the list seemed endless and extended to the open char-a-banc for trips to the seaside. In fact, many cars were not very comfortable, draughty, ice-cold in winter and temperamental at all times, but the cloak of romance covered them all as far as I was concerned, and I longed for the time when I would have one and be able to drive.

~ Vic's bus ignominiously broke down ~

When I was a little lad holidays were taken at places like Skegness, Mablethorpe and Yarmouth, eminently suited to the building of sand castles and paddling. I have vague memories of piers and the delightful penny in the slot machines where little figures enacted the 'Haunted House', 'the Execution, 'the Drunkard in the Graveyard' and other edifying episodes. A donkey ride, Punch and Judy, an ice-cream, I was easily satisfied. We also went to Blackpool when I was about five. Sad to relate, I have no memory of my shameful misbehaviour there, when apparently I ran away from Dad amid the crowds and traffic. It was a very hot day, Dad weighed seventeen stone and lacked mobility. Had he been playing against a Welsh threequarter he could hardly have fared worse. His turning circle was too large, and to the amusement of the holiday crowd, he just could not lay an exasperated hand on me, as, gurgling with delight, I ducked and weaved. I thought it a super game, but when he did finally effect a capture and I was lugged back to the boarding house, I had great difficulty in being thankful for what I received. The boarding houses we patronised were pretty undistinguished and usually had just one bathroom, so once a family got possession it stayed there until the guard was changed, the password being 'Is that you?' 'Yes, it's me'.

Neither of my parents was interested in travel. My mother was content to have a change from housekeeping, my father, who could never sit still for long, went for little walks and little drinks. Only once did we venture up-market, going to a good hotel in Brighton, which even had a tennis court. I can't think how we ever paid for it. As far as I was concerned, it was a flop since the shingle beach was no good for anything. I can still remember the fat, bejewelled Jewish ladies who seemed to play cards all day. On the way we passed through London and I met my father's elder brother, Uncle Tom, for the first time. I wasted no time putting my foot in it. 'Kiss your Uncle Tom, Reggie'. 'I don't like men with moustaches', said I loudly and firmly, glaring at the walrus-like appendage. Mercifully, he had a forgiving nature and when I was ten years old I went to stay with him in Kensington. The contrast could hardly have been greater. To look out of the windows of a fourth floor flat over acres of roofs and chimney pots was an adventure in itself, but paled into insignificance against the fantastically different life-style. Aunty Clarry, his second wife, was totally unorganised. Meal times were at no fixed hour, the whim of the moment was cheerfully acted upon, nobody said, 'do this, don't do that'. I also couldn't stop looking around for my parents when people addressed them as Mr. and Mrs. Woodward. Uncle Tom played the organ at a cinema in Shepherd's Bush and took me along, a young lady neighbour took me to the Zoo, my cousin Freda, a nurse, turned up on her day off and took me to Madame Tussaud's. We travelled on the tube, visited the usual sights, and I went to bed when I felt like it.

~ I was easily satisfied ~

We went somewhat further afield as I grew older. I must have been about twelve when we went to Bridlington. I can remember a steamer trip to Flamborough Head, which was a great thrill until I became distinctly queasy on the way back. I was on my own; Dad had chickened out and nothing would ever have induced Mum to set foot on a boat, in fact merely looking at one bobbing up and down gently made her unwell.

The next year, and the one after, we went to Cheltenham, renting a house in Royal Crescent which belonged to a Miss Woodward, no relation, who had a Dancing Academy, and for whom my mother had worked, playing the piano, before she married. The weather was very hot, which was just as well, because my mother had always cooked on gas, and was deeply suspicious of, and almost totally defeated by, an electric cooker. The hills around were gorgeous. Cleeve Hill, Leckhampton, Seven Springs, and Robinswood Hill at Gloucester; I tramped up and down and across them, entranced by the lovely views over to the Malverns, walked over to Winchcombe and back, and best of all went to the Cheltenham Festival where I saw County Cricket for the first time. I saw my heroes, the Lancashire team, in the flesh, watched Hammond and Paynter make centuries, and was much distressed when Lancashire lost. We went over to Gloucester on the little Great Western line and I explored the Cathedral where my grandfather had sung for nearly forty years, saw the house my father lived in as a boy, and renewed my acquaintance with my mother's cousin, Aunty Nellie, and her elderly father. They were very well off, Uncle John having been the landlord of the Midland Hotel, Gloucester. I marvelled at the readiness of grownups to take offence at virtually nothing. My mother was never at ease there, and when a few months before I had stayed there on my own, I was given a great quantity of advice and instruction on how to behave. Strangely it wasn't at all necessary. I got on fine with my elderly relations and liked them very much.

A school friend, Tom Smith, had recently moved to Cheltenham Grammar School, his father becoming landlord of the village inn at Guiting Power. I stayed there for a day or two, the first time I lived in a small village. It was a new world and full of interest, the rich speech of the villagers, the leisurely pace of life, a real forest in Guiting Wood, the little Cotswold streams.

I managed to get my father to go on a coach trip to Chepstow, Tintern and the Wye Valley. The world was obviously an astonishingly beautiful place and I busied myself finding out more of what it had to offer. Next year at Blackpool Dad and I went on a trip to Windermere and I saw the Lakes for the first time. I determined I would return and climb these marvellous mountains. My parents were totally opposed; to them mountains were objects of fear, people fell off, broke limbs, got lost, perished in snowdrifts, and much more.

The following Easter we went to Scarborough for a week, and I explored the lovely coastline to the north. Robin Hood's Bay was my favourite, though Whitby, with its brownsailed fishing boats huddled under the great hill crowned by the ruined abbey, ran it close.

The year I took my O. Levels I managed to talk my parents into a fortnight at Torquay. I had had my eyes on 'glorious Devon' for some time and was not disappointed. We stayed up at Babbacombe and for one week I had one of the old 'ten bob' tickets on the railway, and every day set off for some new delight. The wealth of historic buildings in Exeter, the sumptuous cathedral, the railway line along the coast, Salcombe and Bolt Head, the fishing port of Brixham, Plymouth and the Hoe, the edge of Dartmoor and Widdecombe, Totnes and the Dart, what a week it was, how full of the beauties of nature and the splendid works of man. My School Certificate results came through in the middle of all this, and were all I dared hope for, and I even learnt to swim. It was the last holiday my parents and I took together. Our interests were so far apart by now that it was pointless. They were not that keen on holidays, anyhow, so in 1936 I went off on my own. The West Country was so lovely I was keen to go back, and decided on Somerset. A letter to the Head Verger at Wells Cathedral, asking if he could suggest somewhere I might stay, brought a happy conclusion and I spent a fortnight in St. Thomas's Street with Mrs. Cooper and her daughter. This enabled me to visit Bristol, the finest of all large English cities, and to go as far afield as Minehead and watch cricket at Western-Super-Mare.

But it was the north I had set my heart on. At Easter 1937 I spent ten days in Durham and was able to explore the Roman Wall, see Sunderland play football, and visit Hexham and Tynemouth. In the summer I spent a fortnight at Carlisle, an ideal centre, since one week I had a ticket for the Lakes and the other week a different one for the Roman Wall, upper Tyne valleys and the Borders. A Carlisle teacher took me up Great Gable. It was a glorious day and I had never seen anything so beautiful. It was a watershed in my life. Ever since I have loved mountains, and still walk on them, having done three treks in the Himalayas since retirement. I didn't tell my parents too much about it, they would only have worried. I went back the next year for another fortnight and it was just as good. I also saw Queen of the South beat Motherwell 4-3, a fine game and a forerunner of the pleasure I was to get watching the splendid Hibernian side from 1946 to 1953.

It never occurred to me even then that I would ever go outside the British Isles, and I had no conception of the riches of European civilisation and its natural beauties, and could not have envisaged the marvellous opportunities of the last few years, brought about by the development of travel by air. My love of travel was firmly established by the time I left school and has greatly enriched my life ever since.

V

I looked forward to going to school. I did not, in fact, do so until I was seven years of age, being considered too delicate! I envied the lads of my age in their little red caps, going to Miss Wileman's school on Burton Road. Imagine then my horror when I was told that I was about to start school at Chestnut House, a girls' school off Spring Hill, with only two other boys beside myself. I still feel this was a dreadful thing to do to me, since I was deprived of the companionship of lads of my age, and the chance to play games, which I enjoyed so much. Academically, I had no problems, since I was already a fluent reader, and competent enough at other subjects, if a slow writer. I thought playing with plasticene was a load of rubbish and deplorably messy, but the class teacher was kind and encouraging, and lessons were fine. Nonetheless, I looked forward eagerly to emancipation from the monstrous regiment of women, and after four terms this duly came about.

Monks Road School was, in the twenties, a successful primary school, the Head Master, Freddy Oldershaw, being perhaps a martinet, but undoubtedly a just and efficient one. He had a special pocket in his trousers, designed to accommodate his cane, which he used not only for the maintenance of discipline, but also to punish slackness. The 'scholarship' form had to submit every Friday to a test administered by him, and if there were no rewards for excellence there were certainly penalties for anything less than what was considered by authority to be one's best. The staff were good and hardworking. They included 'Proker' Rowe, Ernest Abell who later was to write an admirable book about the history of the city, George Clarke, in charge of the scholarship class, always impeccably dressed and known as 'Donkey' Clarke from his habit of calling people 'silly donkey', and Pete Brothwell who taught science and was a notable swimming instructor, the school producing many fine swimmers. There were also Tommy Pykett who was a well-known Football League referee, and Mrs. Lowe, who wept bitterly on Armistice Day at the two minutes' silence, which brought home to us the awful tragedy of the Great War.

The change from an establishment like Chestnut House was traumatic. The regimentation, the large classes, the importance given to arithmetic, never my strong point – oh! the miseries of long division – some dreadfully dull lessons in geography about rivers, marching up the stairs to classes, all combined to make the transition a strange and painful experience. I had only been there a couple of weeks when two large eleven year olds had a fight in the playground. The custom was for all the kids to gather round, forming a ring and chanting 'Er scrap', short for 'there's a scrap'. To an eight year old they seemed

"Er scrap"

enormous and the fight of unbelievable ferocity. I was quite upset, and greatly relieved when a brave teacher separated them before mayhem became murder! Truly, the process of adjustment to an over-protected child is hard indeed. I spent two terms there and didn't enjoy much of it, though had I gone there in the first place instead of Chestnut House,

Three Generations of Choristers:
REMARKABLE RECORD OF THE WOODWARD FAMILY.

Photo, Hadley and Son.
THE LATE MR. THOS. WOODWARD
Nearly Forty Years in Gloucester Cathedral Choir.

Photo, Walker and Son.
MASTER R. C. WOODWARD
Just Admitted to Lincoln Cathedral Choir.

Photo, Walker and Son.
MR. CHARLES WOODWARD
Forty-six Years a Cathedral Chorister.

things would probably have been quite different. I didn't make many friends there, but this was due to the fact that the majority of the lads lived near the school, whereas I lived a long way off, and twice a day had to go through Minster Yard and the Arboretum and back up the steep hill for lunch and tea, quite a walk for a small boy. In addition, I was told I would not be there for very long, and rigorous terms were laid down as to friendships which excluded all but 'nice' boys.

One day early in September, 1928 my father announced that Dr. Bennett had agreed to test my voice with a view to taking me into the Cathedral choir. So I was marched across the road, shown into his study, where, very ill at ease, I did my best to make suitable piping sounds. I

~ I did my best to produce suitable piping sounds ~

had never before seen a piano with pedals, which he used to practise his organ music, and found it hard to concentrate on my test. I can't feel there was any great merit in my performance, and my acceptance owed much to Dr. Bennett's willingness not to disoblige a lay clerk who had worked with him for thirty years.

Events then moved with startling rapidity, clothes were bought for choir and school, and two days later I entered two new and strange worlds, the choir and Lincoln Grammar School. Since school depended on choir, choir had absolute priority, and as a little citizen of two barely compatible worlds, it was not long before I encountered problems.

The Cathedral was a world of its own, a world of rules and protocol presided over by a hierarchy of clergy, some of whom bore a striking resemblance to the fierce Old Testament prophets of stained glass windows. Every day as I came into the Cathedral I passed the statue of Bishop King. My father didn't have that many good words for the Cathedral clergy, but he expressed great admiration and affection for the Bishop, who was held by many in the highest esteem, and by some to be the nearest thing to a saint they had ever met. There is a delicious story about him, sitting on a seat at Eastbourne and finding it, in his old age,

Doctor Bennett, organist at Lincoln Cathedral 1895-1930.

hard work to get up. A little girl, seeing this, offered to help him. "Thank you, my dear, it is very kind of you, but I think I can manage. I am rather weak in the legs". "Don't worry, sir, you ain't 'alf as drunk as my dad is every night".

If I entered by the magnificent West Front, I passed under the statues of St. Hugh and the swineherd who gave St. Hugh his savings to help build the new Cathedral. Neville Richardson, who lived opposite, tells me that when the wind was in a certain quarter, it used to blow through the swineherd's horn, producing a melancholy note.

For a choirboy, however, the centre of the universe is the organist and choirmaster, and in 1928 this was Doctor Bennett. Dr. Bennett was born at Andover in 1863. He became a chorister at Winchester College, went on to study at the Royal Academy of Music, where he was in time to become Professor of Harmony, and continued his studies in Berlin and Munich, where he was a pupil of Kiel and Rheinberger. He came to Lincoln in 1895 and founded the Musical and Orchestral Societies. A thick set man with a luxuriant moustache, a sense of humour and a violent temper, he carried on an enjoyable war with many of the Cathedral dignitaries. He and Dean Fry once went some years without speaking, communicating only by note. In his early days there was a Triennial Festival with Ely and Peterborough, but Dean Fry abolished this in 1910. Precentors gave and received honourable wounds in their running battles. Precentor Bond said, 'Bennett ought to be a cemetery chaplain'. I wonder why? Ernest Blackie had not been Precentor long before the most stupendous confrontation took place over an anthem by Gounod, which he flatly refused to have ever again in the Cathedral. Cardiac arrest was courted by both sides of the dispute, the good doctor waved his umbrella menacingly, but his wild gesticulations were to no avail. When he arrived the Cathedral School was in Northgate, the schoolroom being the small building on the left at the beginning of Nettleham Road, and each day there was a practice followed by Matins, lasting in all from 8.45 till 11, Evensong being sung every day throughout the year likewise. In 1904 the practice of one day with said services was introduced, and soon after, the granting of a month's holiday in August.

It was Precentor Wakeford who, in 1913, moved the school to the Burghersh Chantry in James Street, involving the Cathedral in a substantial financial loss. A masterful man with little sense of humour, he insisted on all doors being locked once a service had begun. An advanced Anglo Catholic, his stall was next to that of Archdeacon Kaye who was an extreme Protestant! The archdeacon remained in office till he was over ninety. He liked his three months as Canon-in-Residence to be consecutive. At their beginning and end he moved house from Riseholme Rectory on a horse dray with his hip bath on top. When he was very old he got stuck in a snow drift on his way to a service. The Cathedral Constable, Mr. Wheatley, gallantly went to the rescue and got stuck as well. They were eventually recovered and taken home exhausted.

My father was appointed by Doctor Bennett as long ago as 1898. He held the good Doctor in the highest esteem as a musician and I think the sentiments were reciprocal, though this did not prevent occasional rows between them. On one occasion they did not speak to each other for six weeks, then one day at lunch time my father came home and reported that they had met in the street, a handshake signifying the end of that particular little cold war. I was seven at the time and it seemed to be a strange way of going on. Adults were definitely odd. Sometimes I saw Doctor Bennett pass my house on his way to and from the Cathedral, a burly figure, heavily moustached. I was too young at the time to realise that he was not in very good health and that his slow walk reflected the effort it was costing him.

~ Doctor Bennett ~

Doctor Bennett lived in North Place, just across the road from our own house, built in 1908. On Sunday mornings he wore a top hat, morning coat and spats, and carried an immaculately rolled umbrella. The lay clerks wore top hats and frock coats, the boys Eton suits and collars, topped by mortar-boards. When Doctor Bennett arrived in 1895 the organ was still hand blown, by an old man named Tommy Dodds. Doctor Bennett kindly gave him some knickerbockers for which he had no further use and was taken aback to hear 'Thankee kindly, sir. The missis will find 'em very useful in cold weather.' Frankly, I was frightened of him since his fierce rages when anything went wrong were of frequent occurrence. In the Song School he would haul a boy by the collar over the music benches at which we stood and administer a beating with a hard and heavy hand. On one occasion this was administered in error to the wrong boy. A shocked silence followed. Finally we told him so. He roared with laughter and said, "Well, it will do for next time". On one occasion he irrupted into the choir during a service and led out a malefactor by the ear. If a boy did not open his mouth wide enough, a fistful of fingers, tasting of tobacco, were inserted. There is a story, which may well be apocryphal, that in a moment of abstraction, while auditioning a lady for the Music Society, he meted out the same treatment, the withdrawal of his fingers being accompanied by the lady's dentures! Yet all this was balanced by genuine kindness. He gave us sumptuous parties at Christmas and mid-summer, and throughout the summer term opened the grounds of North Place for us to play cricket and tennis. I have vivid memories of his retiring behind the massive house and belting tennis balls over the roof onto the lawn. Any boy who caught one got sixpence, but it was pretty difficult since everybody was trying hard.

The assistant organist was at that time Mr. Francis Woolley. He took the probationers over to the Chapter House most days for instruction, but he was to us a rather colourless figure and we preferred the youthful Clifford Hewis who was then a pupil of Doctor Bennett and went on to serve the Cathedral for over half a century.

The gentlemen of the choir would have delighted any novelist who had the wit to invent them. A splendidly variegated bunch, many of them of thirty years' service, their idiosyncrasies afforded us endless entertainment, their sheer professionalism a standard we envied. There were three of each voice. The basses were Mr. Endersby, Mr. Lofthouse and my father. Mr. Endersby, a very distinguished looking man, had a vast voice, like the Lord thundering out of heaven. Mr. Lofthouse was a Yorkshireman and very proud of it. "Eh lad, 'ast tha never bin to Leeds? Tha doesn't know tha's born". He had trouble with his aspirates and we listened eagerly for the verse in the psalm which he rendered as "Why'op ye so, ye 'igh 'ills? This is God's 'ill". Occasionally he had an argument with his wife, which always ended "Who's maister in this 'ouse, then?" "You are, but I'm nek".

One day Mr. Lofthouse heard strange noises from the tenor standing next to him, during the singing of King in F. A quick sideways glance revealed that the singer's book was upside down. 'Eh, Edward, you want to add a drop more soda water". "Eh, lad, I was born in Yorkshire and I know 'ow to sing!" was his theme song. We listened entranced to his rendering of a certain anthem by Boyce: 'I 'ave surely built thee an 'ouse to dwell in. Be'old the 'eaven and 'eaven of 'eavens cannot contain thee, 'ow much less the 'ouse that I 'ave builded. I 'ave 'allowed this 'ouse.'

My father, unfailingly accurate, a fine sight-reader, completed this trio. The tenors were Mr. John Render, another fine musician, the longest serving lay clerk, whose rendering of the tenor solo in Wesley's 'Wilderness' would move a congregation near to tears. Mr. Render married for the third or fourth time, the anthem on that day was 'This is the record of John.' Mr. Booth was a Pickwickian figure who played the

~Mr. Booth was a Pickwickian figure~

bassoon in the local symphony orchestra, and Mr. Kaye was a gifted organist, who, on rare occasions, played for services. Mr. Booth was the only one of the choirmen I really got to know. He resembled one of the fat jolly monks of advertisements for various wines, and his daily walk from Cheviot Street up the steepest of hills diminished him not at all. One day I was complaining to him about having to learn some poetry for prep. To my amazement he was envious rather than otherwise, told me what enjoyment he got from reading poetry and I ended up lending him my 'Mount Helicon' for the holidays. I enjoyed making music and he used to invite me frequently to his house on Sunday evenings. A whole world of beauty was revealed, the lieder of Schubert, Schumann and Brahms, Vaughan Williams, and a great favourite of both of us, Peter Warlock, as well as a host of other delights. When he felt like a change from singing, he got out his bassoon, a fascinating, slightly comical, instrument, and we continued until it was time for supper. I looked forward to these evenings immensely, and since he was an excellent and sensitive musician, enjoyment and profit went hand in hand. Both he and Doctor Slater were Yorkshiremen and therefore determined characters, which led to an extraordinary episode in the singing of Orlando Gibbon's

The choir of Lincoln Cathedral in 1930. My father is second from the right, and I am third from the right of the front row with Neville Richardson on my right, next to the cope-boys.

beautiful anthem 'This is the record of John', which opens with a lengthy tenor solo. They were unable to agree about the speed, and Mr. Booth, with consummate skill, sang from beginning to end exactly a beat and a quarter behind the organ accompaniment. Neither would give an inch, and we listened fascinated.

The Altos were Mr. Farrar, Mr. Laidler who had a beautiful flute-like tone, and Mr. Hodgson who soon left to go to St. George's Windsor. They were a kindly lot, and we could not but benefit from working with them every day.

The Cathedral Chapter inhabited a much loftier plane. At the head was Dean Fry, a former Head Master of Berkhampstead School, a fierce little man with a massive spade beard, devoted to the Cathedral, for which it might be said he gave his life through his tireless work for its restoration. Dean Fry was a short man and bitterly conscious of the fact. One Assize Sunday it was his unhappy fate to walk in procession by the side of a Judge who stood six feet three inches. 'Oh, why was I not made bigger?', he was heard to exclaim in anguish. He worked tirelessly to raise money for the Cathedral Restoration Fund, and travelled three times to the U.S.A., the last time when he was over eighty. At one Christmas Eve Carol Service his red doctor's gown and patriarchal beard caused a small child to exclaim piercingly, 'Look, Daddy, Father Christmas.'

The Subdean was Jeudwine, whose beautiful reading of the lessons was a feature of the services. Precentor Blackie was the dignitary with responsibility for the choir. I remember vividly a day I spent with him at Rochester, where he became Dean. I was by then at his old college so he had an interest in me, but his kindliness and sense of humour went far beyond the call of politeness. The Archdeacon was Bishop Hine. He had been Bishop of Zanzibar where his Cathedral was built on the site of the former slave market. His sister was Muriel Hine, a well known novelist. He loved cats, and there is a delightful statue of him on the West front of St. Wulfram's Church in Grantham (he was the first Bishop of Grantham), a very good likeness, with a cat playing with the tassel of his cassock girdle. I used to pass it every day on my way to work at The King's School and it kept my childhood memories of him very clear.

The Chancellor was Srawley, a very scholarly man. When Mr. Woolley, who was a close friend of his, left to go to Newark, he gave a party for him and the choir boys. It was quite a revelation. Otherwise contact was minimal; a pity, because some of them had had interesting lives and we could have learnt much from them, but the custom and ideas of the time forbade contact and both parties would have found it difficult to know what to talk about. There were three priest vicars, Canon Scott, who was also Rector of St. Mary Magdalene's, later prepared me for Confirmation and employed me to play the organ at his church for the children's service on Sunday afternoons. He was an accomplished musician, who had, in the past, conducted the annual concert of the

Lincoln Orchestral Society. Canon Foster sang the services beautifully, though as a tiny boy I was greatly puzzled by the final versicle and response, 'O God, make clean our hearts with Eno's'. After a short while I found it was not so. 'O God, make clean our hearts within us' was an emendation I learned to accept. The third member of the team was Canon Hagger, with whose son John I was friendly at school. Both he and Canon Foster had chaplaincies as well, the Prison and the Hospital respectively.

There were two vergers, Mr. Newborn and Mr. Welbourn. Mr. Newborn lived in a house opposite the West Front of the Cathedral and he and his wife looked after the choirboy boarders. For most of my time they were Neville Richardson from Wetherby, and, a year younger, their nephew, Pat. Mr. Welbourn had been employed as a stonemason before he became a verger, and he used to make a yearly pilgrimage to Liverpool to see the great new Anglican Cathedral slowly taking shape and would tell us of its many beautiful features. He loved every stone of it.

When I entered the choir, the choir boys were a mixed bunch, high spirited and, in some cases, pretty wild. The standard of academic achievement was generally low, and there was no certainty that a probationer would graduate into the choir. If, after a year, he was not considered to have made the grade, he left and had to return to his elementary school, as happened to a little lad named Haywood a few months after I joined. In the vestry we were under the charge of Mr. Booth, who had the privilege of awarding black marks for undesirable behaviour, a sufficient quantity of these qualifying the recipient for a painful interview with the Precentor. Much that went on was happily never known to the authorities. For instance, some enterprising characters had discovered how to pick the lock at the top of the stairs beyond the Song School, thus gaining access to the wide reaches of the Triforium, not without peril for those whose head for heights was not good. A few of the boys were from middle class backgrounds, the majority were working class. The four senior boys wore copes and sat at each end of their sides in the choir. As a probationer I sat next to Pat Mohan and looked on with awe as he followed the lessons in a Bible in French. The lads were generally kind to me for my father's sake and I began to learn uneasily how to become a member of a very tightly-knit society. I was acutely conscious that I owed my position to my father, since, though I had inherited his musical ability, I had not unfortunately much of a voice.

The life of a choir boy was very hard in those days. We practised every morning from 8.45 to 9.45, followed on Tuesday and Friday by Matins from 9.45 to 10.30. In the afternoon we practised from 3.45 to 4.30 when we sang Evensong till 5.15. Wednesday was a free day, unless it was a Saint's Day when it would be exchanged with Tuesday. On Sunday we practised at 10.00, sang Matins at 10.30, left before the sermon for a bun and milk in the Song School, sang Choral Eucharist at 11.45 and Evensong at 3.15. We missed seven school lessons a week, had to do the same work as other boys at School, fit in our homework, and accept that we had to work during most of the Christmas and Easter holidays, and had only four weeks holiday in the summer. In the weeks preceding performances of the Messiah and the St. Matthew Passion, we had practices on Monday nights from 7.30 to 9.15, extra evening services in Lent and so on. It was a mile from the Cathedral to the School, as well. Many of the lads had bikes. I did not, I had to walk. One thing must be said. The lad who learns to cope with all this is unlikely to be defeated by anything later on. Lessons for survival are for life. In return, our school fees were paid for us, probationers got ten shillings a quarter, choir boys twenty-five shillings a quarter, which did not even pay for our clothes. The Cathedral did buy us our mortar-boards, which we wore to the Cathedral on Sundays together with Eton jackets, striped trousers and stiff wide collars to match. It is a wonder that any strangulated sounds emerged from our little throats. The Cathedral was often alarmingly cold in the winter, and my years in the choir were the only time in my life that I have suffered from chilblains on my feet. The music was very difficult at times, and I specially dreaded the things we sang from the Boyce books. These were enormous volumes, very heavy, with only the treble part in them. Sometimes we had to count up to fifty bars' rest, with the certainty of a fearful row if we made a false entry.

There were compensations, however. To spend some time each day in one of the most beautiful buildings in the world has an effect on even the most Philistine little soul, and I speedily began to find some of the music a moving experience. I soon outgrew my liking for Goss, preferred Handel to Bach, paid lip-service to Byrd and the music of his day, and enjoyed Stanford enormously. We sang as anthems some of the numbers from Brahms' Requiem, and new horizons appeared. Day by day we sang the Psalms. The words were occasionally incomprehensible, but much of their poetry and view of human life soaked into me. Then the lessons of being part of a highly skilled team, and in due course learning the responsibilities of leadership, were of great value. There were special occasions, too, which were exciting, such as Assize Sunday when the presiding judge, his officers and civic dignitaries, attended in great pomp and circumstance, and we scrutinised the face of a man who might well have to sentence another to death before the week was out. There was the Christmas Carol Service, and the magical moment when we gathered under the sole light of the giant candelabra in the Choir. When we sang the Messiah we were joined by the Lincoln Choral Society and Orchestra, and the thrilling sounds of trumpets and tympani filled the great nave. In the Bach St. Matthew Passion I heard my father sing with great sensitivity the part of Jesus, and listened entranced to the bittersweet notes of the oboe.

These feelings only surfaced occasionally. Small boys don't reflect too much on their existence and, to be honest, we really hadn't time to do so, we were far too busy. It was only later on that we realised the influences that had been at work on us.

VI

Then Doctor Bennett died, Mr. Woolley acted as choirmaster for three months, and we all wondered anxiously who would get the job. It turned out to be Doctor Gordon Slater, who was then only thirty four years of age, so obviously there would be changes. Doctor Bennett had himself been a quirister at Winchester, had grown up in the Victorian age and was an Edwardian at heart and in his musical ideas. His ideas of discipline came from that age, too. We had a lot of adjusting to do.

Doctor Slater arrived and proved to be stout, balding, with a booming laugh. He was quick to voice his appreciation when we did well, equally quick to hold extremely lengthy inquests when things went wrong. He talked to us a lot, since he believed that we would sing best if we thoroughly understood what we were doing. Since his initials were G.A.S. it is not surprising that in no time at all the enterprising had nicknamed him 'Gassy'. His standards were very high, and he took pains to check the academic attainment of those who came for voice trials. The new boys who appeared were often highly intelligent and the choir altered accordingly. We applied ourselves to organising other aspects of life than our singing, and became a formidable unit on the cricket and football fields. Of those who were to all intents and purposes my contemporaries, Tommy Kirkby, Neville Richardson, Tim MacDonald, Geoff Spalding and I all played in due course for the school first eleven at cricket, the first three at football as well, and Neville won the five mile cross-country. There were other useful performers in our team such as Geoff Broxholme, Godfrey Rumsey, Phil Daughton and Dick Rollett. In my last year in the choir we played sixteen cricket matches against teams from our own school and the City School, Newark Parish Choir, the old

Dr. Gordon Slater on his appointment as organist of Lincoln Cathedral in 1930.

choirboys and the workmen engaged in the restoration work of the Cathedral. Doctor Slater encouraged us in this and got the Cathedral authorities to buy us bats, pads and gloves, just as he encouraged us in school work, asking us how the exams. had gone.

When anyone complained about us he always took our part and defended us, unless it was proved beyond doubt that we were wrong. One of his first actions was to abolish the black mark system, replacing it by simple trust. We behaved much better as a result, not liking to let him down. His sense of humour never failed. One April Fool's day Neville reported that he had broken a note playing the piano before the Doctor's arrival. With a serious face Dr. Slater played a chromatic scale the length of the keyboard. Slightly puzzled, he played it again – and a third time. By now we were all a bit worried that we had gone too far. Plucking up his courage, Neville mentioned the date. There was a moment of deathly silence, then he roared with laughter. One day he was quite late for practice, an exceedingly rare event. His assistant had not turned up either and eventually Ken Senior suggested I take the practice. Everything was in full swing when he arrived, tip-toeing into the room so as not to disturb anyone. His look of amazement when he reached the keyboard and found me playing was truly comical. He was highly delighted and from then on Basil Pearce and I alternated in taking the practice on one afternoon each week.

A few weeks after Dr. Slater's arrival a new assistant appeared, a Lancastrian, Doctor Willis Grant. He was only in his early twenties, very energetic, and played cricket with us sometimes. In later life he became Professor of Music at Bristol University. They made a powerful team, and the winds of change swept through the Cathedral, at times approaching gale force. Some items vanished from the repertoire, and I missed some of the expansive high Victorian and Edwardian services such as Smart in B flat, and Bennett in A. The music of modern composers such as Darke and Vaughan Williams made an appearance and I didn't like it much at first. Gradually, however, I began to appreciate it, and the marvellous unaccompanied second section of 'Lord, thou hast been our refuge' was a stunning and quite new experience. The Messiah was now sung on alternate years only, Bach's Christmas Oratorio being added. I liked it very much, though the Messiah was still my favourite. My musical appreciation was growing all the time, since Doctor Slater spent quite a lot of time talking to us, getting us to think about the words we were singing, to understand what the composer was doing, to listen to the whole effect and not just our treble part. At first we thought this was all just wasting time, but slowly we began to appreciate his concern that we should understand and reflect upon what we were doing. This approach made life harder, we could no longer just sing, disciplined concentration was needed, but it gave meaning to all we did. The simple things were meticulously practised, the Psalms and the Responses, and some of them were deeply moving such as the Russian Kontakion for the departed, from the English Hymnal, on All Souls' Day.

In those days a boy's voice lasted until fifteen, often sixteen and occasionally seventeen, so there was always a lot of experience at the top end of the choir. Nowadays, with much earlier maturity, the oldest boy is likely to be only thirteen, which places much responsibility on one so young. A choirboy is a professional at a very early age, singing works, some of which are of great difficulty and complexity, in company with adults who are giving a large part of their life to music and are in some cases highly qualified academically. He is a child doing a man's work in a man's world. It is not surprising that cathedral choirboys are so commonly successful in adult life. By the age of eleven they have learnt to survive and tackle a hard job successfully.

In five and a half years I sat through stacks of sermons. I was quite willing to listen and tried to do so, but the majority were so far over my head that I was soon defeated and turned to the contemplation of the beauties of the architecture of the Angel Choir or to a consideration of the next football or cricket match. Help was never far away. It was reliably reported that if the preacher went on too long Mr. Newborn the head verger would steal out and begin switching on the lights. 'Finally, dear brethren' wasn't long in coming then.

After Dean Fry died, he was succeeded by Dean Mitchell, who, one Sunday morning, informed us that he could best think of God as a shapeless white mass. Since I believed I had pretty reliable information that he was old and with a white beard, a sort of larger edition of Dean Fry, I could barely believe my ears at such scandalous heresy from one who should surely know better. I consulted my father, who wisely didn't often bother to listen to sermons, and got little comfort. He didn't really relish a theological discussion on the being of God and the Dean's copybook remained blotted in my little eyes.

Some things did not escape my father's sharp eyes, however, such as the Canon who wore a very long hood into which he had subtly introduced a small cushion to make his hard stall more bearable and he told me stories about the choirmen of times past. One of them was a great practical joker. His name was Sedgwick, he was distinguished by a shock of wild hair, a red face and a perpetual grin. A slightly doddery canon residentiary used to go into the men's vestry from time to time and bore them to tears. On one occasion, seeing him coming, this choirman quickly shut himself in one of the cupboards containing cassocks and surplices, and made scratching noises on the woodwork. There was no question of not hearing them and the poor old canon expressed great concern that there should be rats in the vestry. The men were hard put to maintain suitable decorum. On another occasion his victim was an irascible verger named Logsdail. It was the custom for the canon in residence to be met before a service at the West Front, and preceded to the Clergy vestry all the way up the Nave and choir aisle by a verger with his silver wand, (usually referred to by my father as his poker). On this day, barely had they started than the canon saw someone he wanted to speak to, and turned aside, all unkown to Logsdail, who proceeded on his way, unconscious that his place had been taken by a grinning choirman who swept pompously along behind him. At the clergy vestry the verger turned to accord the usual civility of a bow, which was returned with due solemnity. He could barely restrain himself from assault and battery with the aforesaid poker, and passionately uttered words which I cannot with decency chronicle, except to say that they were of Anglo-Saxon origin and few letters.

The treble section of a Cathedral choir renews some part of itself every year. We had four cope boys, sixteen Burghersh chanters (a fine name for the rank and file) and up to six probationers. In some cases the children of the lay clerks became choirboys, and Eric Rumsey and his younger brother Godfrey were my friends before I joined the choir. Eric played all games well, being what in these days would be called a real competitor. He was about eighteen months older than me, so I looked up to him and set great store by what he told me about both choir and school. Harold Morton, who had an older brother George, also befriended me. I still remember that at the age of ten he wore a Labour rosette at the general election of 1929, which must have taken some doing in the Prep, since everybody else was Conservative or Liberal. Basil Pearce arrived soon after me and we became friends, being in the same form all the way up the School to School Certificate. He was the ablest musician of my contemporaries and eventually made it his career. He was a gifted organist and we spent hours together in the organ loft of St. Mary Magdalene's Church. Geoff Broxholme, whom I had known at Monk's Road School, came at the same time and sang in the choir till he was seventeen! He won the Victor Ludorum in the Prep in 1930. Neville Richardson came from Wetherby to board with the Newborns'. He was a bright lad and a year ahead of me at school. It was through Neville more than anyone that I began to join in football as well as cricket. I was considered a somewhat delicate child, football was rough and meant getting dirty and wet, so parental authority was against it. By the age of eleven I realised that since I got colds anyhow, I might as well have my fun, so I played, and my health improved dramatically.

Tommy Kirkby I had also known before he joined the choir. He was a fine games player, and on one occasion the victim of a shocking tragedy. He was the only one among us fortunate enough to possess his own cricket bat, and soon after he had it the handle came clean out in the course of a majestic stroke, being left in his hand, while the rest of the bat made mid-on run for his life. We thought it a huge joke at first, but such was his sorrow that we soon began to feel ashamed of ourselves. Ken Parker had the best solo voice in my time in the choir, a fine rich sound. Tim Macdonald came all the way from Swanpool and it must have been a hard life for him. He was another fine all-round games player. In those days the school-leaving age was fourteen and several of those who were in the choir when I joined left school when they left the choir and got jobs and the personnel of the choir was changing rapidly. Some of the little lads who arrived about 1931 were very bright, notably Peter Harker, who later went to Canada with a string of degrees to his name. When I left the choir in 1934 my place was taken by Dennis Townhill, who is now the organist and choirmaster of St. Mary's Cathedral, Edinburgh, a remarkable coincidence since I was Head Master of its Choir School from 1948 to 1953.

Each year the Old Choristers had a Reunion and used to invite us to tea at the White Hart, along with the lay clerks. There were some colourful characters among them, and some famous names, like Webster Booth the singer, and the writer Basil Boothroyd. After tea there were songs by those prepared to take part. My most vivid memory is of Mr. Endersby singing superbly a well known Victorian ballad called 'Leaning'. Doctor Slater continued the custom of giving us a fine Christmas party, and each year we had a cricket match with Newark Parish Church Choir, where Mr. Woolley was choirmaster. At one of these they challenged each other to a hundred yard race, which to our amazement Doctor Slater won, for he was very, very heavy.

The Song School at Lincoln is, in fact, over the clergy vestry, up a winding turret staircase. It contained a small organ which was never used, a grand piano serving for practice. We stood for practice at high wooden music benches on either side of the piano, the men sat behind us for the two full practices on Tuesday and Friday mornings. For the remainder of the week we practised on our own, the eldest boys towering over the benches, the youngest peering under them. In the morning our little pipes were opened by singing exercises, scales, arpeggios, and a sustaining exercise which we sang to 'moo-moh-mah-may-me!' The music was laid out for the week by Mr. Lofthouse on a large table and the appropriate items taken down for the services as they became due. Psalters, chantbooks, hymn books and any new or special music was also to hand. The old Psalters in use when I first joined the choir had the numbers in Roman numerals, and to be told to turn up Psalm LXXXIX for instance, was a sore trial for newcomers. There was a small urinal outside the foot of the stair, anything more necessitated a trip right across the cathedral to the cloisters and was good for up to ten minutes' absence, a fact of which the enterprising made full use on occasion. The stairway to the Song School was both long and steep, so it was quite easy to hear authority puff and pant its way up, allowing for any nefarious activities to be terminated in plenty of time.

Our vestry was opposite the men's vestry, separated by the width of the transept. We wore black cassocks in those days, ruffs being added, to our great disgust, soon after Doctor Slater came, surplices of about knee length, and the four headboys wore fine black copes with a light grey border and modestly decorated crosspiece. A few years later the congregation was treated to an incredible coincidence, since the headboys were respectively the Taylor twins and the Rushton twins, identical except on very close inspection. It is said that more than one sinner promised that he would never touch another drop, after being subjected to such a sight! Occasionally we caught a glimpse across a passage of the solemnities of the clergy vestry and wondered whatever they found to talk about. They may have been less remote from life than they seemed, for both Canon Scott and Dean Mitchell liked to go to Sincil Bank to see Linclon City play football. When the bell struck we poured out from our respective vestries, our faces arranged in suitably holy expressions, and, I fear, shambled off down the aisle, cutting the corners untidily. Doctor Slater soon put a stop to that. We didn't enjoy the practice walks he made us do, but we got the message. The final vestry prayer was followed by a ceremonial bow in the direction of the senior dignitary present, which was returned with reasonable civility. No word was ever uttered and a few years later at Edinburgh I though how gracious by comparison was Provost Ramsay's smiling 'Thank you, gentlemen. Thank you, boys', after every service.

To the young, adults easily tend to seem old, anyhow, but in 1928 three of the Cathedral dignitaries were in their late seventies, Doctor Bennett was sixty five, and five of the choirmen were in their middle fifties, so it is not surprising that we felt those around us were old, lived in a different world from us, and didn't easily understand what life was like at our level. People considered themselves to be old in those days when they reached their late forties and behaved accordingly. They moved sedately, never hurrying. Society has changed greatly in this respect over the last twenty years, people expect to live longer and do so, and they remain active and younger in outlook to a far greater age. Communication across the generations is much more open, and the dismantling of many of the barriers of class has helped greatly towards this. Choirboys of today would generally have to make a big effort of imagination to picture how things were then. Authority was all-powerful and often remote, too, and it was accepted in a way it would never be today.

Broadcasting was relatively in its infancy, and though we made one or two broadcasts, they were a rare event and did not impinge much on the daily routine. No one had thought of making and selling gramophone records of cathedral music, and not until the coming of the long playing records was this a viable proposition. Unhappily, therefore, I have no record of the choir of my day, nor do I have a record of my father's voice, which I would have liked very much.

I think most of us preferred singing in the choir to singing in the nave. The lighting was very poor in both places and on a dark winter evening it was easy to misread a note or two. There was, fortunately, no decorative scroll ironwork for us to fiddle with. On one occasion at Edinburgh as I was singing the prayers after the anthem, I became aware of a subdued snivelling to my left. A quick glance revealed that young Alan had wriggled his finger into a small hole, and the united efforts of himself and the boys either side of him were unable to get it out. The sounds of distress grew minute by minute, and at the conclusion of the service the boys on that side had to perform the not inconsiderable gymnastic feat of vaulting over him to make their exit, abandoning the lonely little figure to his imprisonment. After the vestry prayer, a rescue party of men and boys set off hot foot, but, by this time, wasted by suffering, he had just managed to effect his own relief.

On the rare occasions when we sang out of doors – funerals, the impressive Good Friday procession of witness for instance – the choirmen had little round black skull caps and we had, as best we could, to stifle our laughter at the comical figure some of them cut. Very funny things happen in Cathedrals, and at a Confirmation in Edinburgh a lady of riper years was walking up the nave for the Bishop to lay his hands on her, perhaps it would be better to say administer the rite, when the vicious wind which was a permanent resident of the Cathedral, whipped her long veil across her face. She was temporarily blinded, the senior verger sprang gallantly to the rescue, but unhappily ten seconds of his ministrations were sufficient to reduce the poor woman to a cross between an Egyptian mummy and a Christmas parcel. It took three people to disentangle her by which time the Bishop's blood pressure had mounted alarmingly.

On Sunday mornings when I first joined the choir we had to go to the Precentor's house where he gave us some religious instruction. Sometimes he was away, or ill, so that week we did not go. Then the blow fell. The authorities decided that for our good we should attend Sunday School at St. Mary Magdalene's church with Canon Scott at 2.15 every Sunday afternoon. This was considerably more than another straw on an already overloaded camel's back, and though Canon Scott called it his Junior Congregation, we knew a Sunday School when we saw one. There we made the acquaintance of a remarkable elderly lady named Miss Kennedy who lived in James Street nearby, and used to invite the choirboys three at a time to tea. She had more understanding of small and medium-sized boys than we would ever have expected. We did not exactly look forward to going at first, but soon swallowed our doubts. Her house is now a boarding house for the Cathedral Choir School and I think she would have liked that very much. Also in James Street lived Canon Jarvis, and he entertained us, too. He had a beautiful lawn, one of the finest I have ever seen outside the Oxbridge Colleges, on which we played croquet and enjoyed it, in spite of suspicions that it was hardly a manly pastime. He had a fine library and used to lend me books, a privilege that I valued greatly. His house was the Burghursh Chantry from which we choirboys took our title. He had gained a rowing blue at Oxbridge and had the oar over his mantelpiece.

We had to follow the lessons in the Bibles provided for us and sometimes comics were surreptitiously slipped between the pages. Finally someone was caught doing this by Dean Fry, no less, and there was the most dreadful row, the culprit coming very close to expulsion. When I first joined the choir several of the lads were expert at the deaf and dumb sign language, which was safer than whispering, but a very cumbersome method of communication.

In the holidays the verger could be prevailed upon to unlock the door to let us go up the central tower, either on our own or in a little group. This was a coveted privilege and no one ever abused it. It was a fascinating world up there, and the sound of the great bell striking the hour was quite awe-inspiring if you were in the bell chamber at the time. When the summit was reached, there was our fair city spread out below us. I used to look eagerly for my own house, quite close below, then at the fine gardens of many of the Minster Yard properties, which we never saw at ground level, at the green countryside not so far away as it is now, at the tight packed rows of houses round the factories downhill and gaze earnestly into the distance in case it was one of those rare days when Boston Stump, thirty miles away, was visible. Immediately below, a sea of grey lead roof covered the lovely building where we worked. For three years large parts of it, both inside and out, were covered in wooden scaffolding as urgent and extensive restoration work was carried out, and a small army of stonemasons worked in huts erected in the grounds on the north side of the nave. The service of Thanksgiving at the conclusion of all this, was attended by the Duke and Duchess of York, who were to become King and Queen a very few years afterwards.

~ Very self conscious indeed ~

My last year in the Cathedral Choir, one of the cope-boys, in 1933.

Every year we had free seats for the Lincoln Orchestral Society's concerts in the Corn Exchange, and had to go whether we wanted to or not. Symphonic music was quite unfamiliar to me, since we had neither wireless nor gramophone at home. In my last year in the choir Doctor Slater asked me to play the big bass drum in Schubert's Marche Militaire. Very self conscious indeed, I had to fetch it and carry it down the High Street. The rehearsal went badly since I gained a public rebuke for being behind the beat, a fact of which I was quite unconscious. I was in a state of panic on the night and banged the wretched thing in a refined mixture of despair and hope. A public commendation next morning at practice made some amends for shattered nerves.

As we progressed up the choir we were given the responsibility of looking after the younger boys and I enjoyed the lively friendliness of small boys like Charlie Mansford and Dick Scott. By 1934, however, I felt I had both given and taken as much as was possible from the choir, and I was anxious to spend my time on the qualifications needed for a career and to take a full part in the wider world of school. All partings are a wrench, I was leaving something that had been priority number one in my life since the age of nine. Some of my friends would be remaining in the choir for a year or two, and I knew I would miss Doctor Slater whom I had come to like and respect enormously. Even fifty years later, I don't find it easy to make up a profit and loss account for these years.

VII

The grammar school in the late twenties contained a Preparatory Department of about forty five boys and a main school of some two hundred pupils. The Head Master was Dr. Moxon of whom I have little clear recollection. I was handed over to him by my father, and I remember walking behind his gowned figure down a long corridor on the way to the Prep. It would never have occurred to him that a little boy would have been grateful for a friendly word or two about no matter what. When he came to the School in 1911 there were only fifty eight boys, when he left there were two hundred and fifty three. Three members of staff had been at the school throughout his headship, Messrs. Mence, Withers and Plant. For Morning Assembly, Dr. Moxon wore cassock, gown and square, and the service consisted of General Confession, Absolution, Lord's Prayer, Collect or Grace, Prayer of St. Chrysostom and the Grace. There were prayers at 3.30 also, which we choirboys did not attend, being on the way to practice at the Cathedral. These were abolished by Mr. Young. In 1928 the School had gained six Higher (A. Level) School Certificates, and twenty five School (O. Level) Certificates. There were thirty five boys in the sixth form. In 1929 there were only four A's and fifteen O's, and in 1930 4 A's and 17 O's. Many boys were presumably leaving during their sixth form course. For Highers it was necessary to do two main and two subsidiary subjects. For School Certificate passes were needed in English, Maths., a language and two others. The pass mark was 35%, and 45% gained a credit. Five

Lincoln School Prep. 1930.
I didn't wear my cap in bed,
but I was proud of it!

Our house in Nettleham Road.

credits brought exemption from London Matriculation and had to include Latin as well as English and Maths.

Every day after assembly boys queued up to present the Head Master with notes explaining absence or requesting leave off games and 'gym' as P.E. was then called. Assembly was held in the room at the west end of the cloisters, which later became the woodwork room. The sixth form stood at the front, the Prep. at the back, form masters with their forms. In 1928 there was a weekly class order and the first boy had to go up and fetch it from the Head Master. For the rest of the day this room acted as the gymnasium.

School uniform existed, but was not compulsory. It consisted of grey flannel trousers, a black blazer with blue piping and a blue and black tie. If you got colours, you put them on your blazer. Some lads wore suits, some grey flannels with variegated ties. Choir boys had to wear out their Sunday clothes before they became too small, which we hated. Younger boys commonly wore wellingtons, or gumboots as they were called, in wet weather. Only caps were obligatory; prefects had elegant tassels to add to them.

The Prep., an old World War One army hut, contained three forms and I was given into the charge of Mr. Withers, form master of the first form. He had spent most of his life at the school, as pupil and teacher and gave great service to the Old Boys' Society. He was to live to a very advanced age, retained his interest in the School to the last and left a large sum of money with which the splendid outdoor swimming pool was built. Grey haired, with a little bristling moustache, he rejoiced in the

~ fruity and wide ranging aroma of pipe tobaccos ~

nickname of Stinker, thanks to the fruity and wide-ranging aroma of pipe tobacco which went before him. Despite a reputation for uncertain temper, he was kindly and appreciative of effort. For most of the week the three Prep. masters took their own forms, though for one or two periods they might swap. I found work in form one easy and enjoyed most of it. I hated writing lessons. Always a slow writer, I found the copperplate examples most difficult to imitate and the process was not helped by the dulness of the subject matter, the most interesting sentences only rising to the heights of 'The Severn is the longest river in England' or 'A stitch in time saves nine'. Most of us did not have fountain pens and dipped our pens in the inkwells contained in every desk.

I loved reading and occasionally we were allowed to take one of a fine collection of boys' books from a wire-fronted, padlocked, bookcase for a reading period. At last I screwed my courage to the sticking point and asked if a book might be borrowed for home reading. The answer was predictable and the cause of some unhappiness and frustration.

At the end of the term Mr. Withers told me that I was to go to 2B after the Christmas holidays. I was naturally elated, but visions of a distinguished academic career soon melted away. Very quickly I had to come to terms with the fact that many members of staff looked down upon choirboys, a view faithfully reflected by some of the boys. There were, perhaps, at any one time, five or six of us choirboys in the Prep, we were the only boys whose parents did not pay fees, some of us came from homes where money was scarce, and one boy's father was known to vote Labour! Further, in any one week we missed at least seven periods for our singing activities, so we always had to struggle to keep up with our work. The form master of 2B was Charlie Watts, short, with a little dark moustache, a schoolboyish sense of humour and an interest in Elizabethan music. As a choirboy I was under contract to tell him when Byrd's 'Ave Verum' was being sung. Later I came to know him as a gentle soul, lacking in self-confidence. Soon after the war he died as a result of taking an overdose of sleeping pills, whether in momentary confusion in the middle of the night or in horror at the dissolution of the Prep. and the necessity of teaching older boys, who can tell? It must be said that he was inclined to have his little favourites among his pupils and was not very good at showing interest in the rest. My particular problem was French. The rest of the form had already been doing it for a term and knew something. I knew nothing. My difficulties could have been speedily resolved by a little help and explanation. As it was, I was left to sink and did so with barely a protesting gurgle.

The end of term produced a disagreeable shock in the shape of a 'holiday task'. Each holiday we had to read a book and do an exam. on it the first day of the following term. This one was 'The Voyages of Sir Francis Drake'. At ten years old I had barely heard of South America and the Spanish names were fiendishly difficult to remember. Conscientious little idiot that I was, I read it carefully twice, probably the only boy to do so. Each form master chose the books for his form. Some of them, in after years, were 'The Black Arrow', 'Silas Marner', 'Tanglewood Tales', 'The First Man in the Moon', 'The Food of the Gods'. I gained the Scripture Prize that year. It was commonly felt that my daily

Mr. C. E. Young, Headmaster of Lincoln School 1929-1937.

exposure to Holy Writ gave me an unfair advantage, and it didn't increase my popularity with my fellows, the word 'Swot' being liberally applied. I hadn't any real friends in the form and was very uncomfortable.

In the Prep. games were played in school time, but in the main school they were played after afternoon school twice a week and were compulsory. This meant that choirboys in the main school could not take part in normal school games and there was little prospect of playing for a school team. There was little attempt at coaching, but little lungs were filled with fresh air, even if little shins were hacked. However, the summer term brought cricket instead of football, and that was some consolation. One afternoon I hit the stumps nine times, incredible really since my action was nonsensical – I bowled round the back of my head and couldn't see the stumps when I was delivering the ball. The following summer I took up wicket keeping. Cricket balls were hard and hurt my hands. I reckoned I'd be better off with thick gloves.

I very much wanted to learn to swim, but the swimming pool was in a sunless corner behind the cloisters and fearfully cold, and not until I was sixteen did I achieve my objective. In 1928, out of 48 boys in the Prep., fourteen were able to swim a length and Mr. Watts reported that the water was 'thick and green'. I duly received my prize at Speech Day from the hands of the Dean, Dr. Fry. I sang to him every day in the Cathedral, but there was not a flicker of recognition in his eye. If he realised I was one of his choristers, which I very much doubt, he was not prepared to show it.

Form 2A was under the command of Mr. Marriott, who, as a former useful cricketer with the Lindum, started quite high on my list. He was, however, aloof, not communicating easily with any of us, though I was very interested when he told me that he gave up playing cricket when he was unable to field as well as he would have liked. Among other things he introduced us to grammar, parsing and analysis. I was bewildered by it all, especially clauses, but the educational process was beginning and I was by now organised enough to sit next to someone who was good at it. My friendships were, and remained for the next four years, with other choirboys rather than with other members of my form, Basil Pearce, with whom I had strong common musical interests and Tommy Kirkby, with whom I exchanged copies of the Magnet and the Gem. The world of Greyfriars seemed a long way from reality as experienced in 2A, but it made for a lot of enjoyment. We also started Latin that year, and surprisingly I did quite well at it. Like most lads, I did not question the usefulness of what I was taught. If modest success was achieved, that was fine by me.

The year passed reasonably; if not enthusiastically happy, I was certainly not miserable, but the loss of so many periods for Choir duties made the work at school a constant struggle. We had a new Head Master at the beginning of the year, Dr. Moxon being succeeded by Mr. Young.

It didn't seem to make much difference to life in 2A. In later years at school, I came to know him well and owed him much for his kindness and encouragement. He was only thirty four at the time of his appointment and it took both staff and boys some time to realise that the Governors had made an excellent choice. All this, however, lay in the future. Mr. Young began his first day with a service in the Cathedral, followed by an assembly in the gymnasium at which he called the school roll, every boy having to answer 'present'. Health Certificates, certifying that the pupil had been in contact with no infectious diseases were handed in to Form masters, followed by a kit inspection, games kit, cap, coat, scarf, all of which had to be correctly marked with the owner's name. The afternoon was given over to an exam. on the Holiday Task. The next day saw the introduction of a hymn at assembly. Mr. Young had been sixth form master at Fettes in Edinburgh, and in Scotland boys were men. He apparently wanted all masters to have a cane in the room and use it!

Each term now began with a service in the Cathedral, the date being carefully arranged so that it was a day earlier or later than that of the nearby Girls' High School, so that boys and girls should never meet, and youthful passions be aroused. The service was not very inspiring, but one term it was redeemed when Bishop Hine, in his sermon, asked a rhetorical question, and to the delight of all, Hayes Hind, then in his second year, leapt to his feet, with hand up, determined to answer. 'Sir! Sir!' Very impressive, however, was the service of Armistice Day, the forerunner of Remembrance Sunday. Yellow and white chrysanthemums in pots were placed at the foot of the war memorial in the cloisters. At 10.50 the bell was rung and the whole school assembled in the gymnasium. The lesson was read by Jazzy Lee, the School Captain read a list of the Old Boys who had given their lives in the War, the Lord's Prayer was followed by prayers read by the Head Master. We listened for the Cathedral bell to strike eleven, then there was the two minutes' silence, the wind blowing round the building, the ill-fitting door rattling, the creak of leather as boys shifted their feet. A factory hooter signalled the end of the silence, succeeded by an outburst of coughing and throat clearing. The proceedings ended with the hymn 'O valiant hearts' and the National Anthem.

Speech day was another great day, with Hatton's big marquee dispensing teas at a shilling a head, and Mr. Young replendent in frock coat and top hat. The new pavilion was opened on Speech Day, 1931.

I entered the main school in September, 1930, at the age of eleven, and was at once in a different world. The School was organised so that the boys from the Prep. went into 3B and the bulk of the scholarship boys into 3A. Most of these proceeded to the School Certificate in four years, the remainder taking five. There were Christ Hospital Scholarships and City scholarships. At the beginning of term Text books were issued by Miss Footman, the school secretary. To the fascinated amazement of little lads from homes where circumstances were straitened, they found themselves referred to as 'scholars', and issued with new text books, while the children of the relatively affluent were labelled 'commoners' and received books which might fairly be described as multiple-hand rather than second-hand.

I met again some lads whom I had known two years earlier at Monks Road School. The biggest change was that instead of a form teacher who taught us most things, we now had to adjust to specialist teachers and might meet seven different men in one day. In those days many masters had to fill up their time-table by teaching another subject. The newly-appointed Chemistry master taught us the Geography of North America, the senior Maths. teacher instructed us in essay writing. Algebra bewildered me, but otherwise there were no serious problems and I stayed around the middle of the form. Mr. Young had made one important change to the time-table which made life much easier for the choirboys. Instead of missing periods in several subjects, we now dispensed with one subject altogether, Latin being time-tabled for when we were at the Cathedral.

Even so, life was uncomfortably busy. We had school till lunch time on Saturday, practised at the Cathedral every morning except Wednesday, sang Matins twice a week afterwards and Evensong every afternoon except Wednesday. Three services on Sunday and the week began again. We were on duty during most of the Christmas and Easter holidays and half of the summer holidays. There were extra evening practices for performances of the Messiah, Christmas Oratorio and the St. Matthew Passion and it was hard to do homework on top of all this. I was now realising that at the end of the road a dragon lay in wait in the guise of the School Certificate. Pat Mohan was the first choirboy to take this successfully, soon followed by Tom Daniels, but most choirboys left for employment before taking it, at any age after fourteen, which was the school-leaving age then, as did quite a lot of fee-paying pupils, and by and large the staff did not think in terms of success at this level for choirboys. The summer exams. found me marginally over the halfway mark in the two forms put together, so I was destined for 4A with the bright lads from among the scholarship boys, a sure recipe for disaster.

The next year was the most miserable of my school life. I would have been stretched to the limit without the choir work and with it I simply foundered. I took refuge in psycho-somatic illness, thereby making my troubles infinitely worse. My reports were full of doom-laden prophecy ('generally lacking in effort and interest'), my parents thundered away and threatened me with boarding. I didn't realise how empty the threat was, since they couldn't have afforded it. I made feeble promises of amendment, which I was incapable of fulfilling.

Some of the work I enjoyed. I met John Phillips for the first time and greatly enjoyed the Shakespeare plays which we boisterously acted on the floor in front of the desks. French I feared. I didn't understand it

~ *which we boisterously acted* ~

and had the misfortune to encounter a fierce young man in his first year of teaching, Mr. Axton. He genuinely got into fearsome rages, red as a turkey-cock being no exaggeration. "For the Lord's sake say something!", he yelled at me. I would gladly have obliged him, but the Lord put no words into my mouth.

Scripture was the province of the only clergyman on the staff, Jazzy Lee, who also taught middle school maths. A north countryman, he had been a fine games player. A very sarcastic man, he couldn't stand Mr. Dollery, and egged on by the boys would declare he could bowl him with a football. He was far from prompt in appearing at lessons and his first remark was frequently, 'Has Charterhouse and Exeter been in?'. We were thoroughly mystified by this, until one bright lad discovered from the School Prospectus that that was where the Head Master had been educated. Jazzy's opinions were well left of centre and sometimes he set us work, then retired ostentatiously behind the pages of the Daily Herald. Like four or five of the staff, he was a regular attender at Sincil Bank, and it was often possible on a Monday morning to avoid work for quite a bit of the period by ensnaring him into a discussion of the deeds and misdeeds of the Lincoln City players on the previous Saturday. About the year 1932 Lincoln City had a very good centre-forward named Alan Hall, sold the following year to Spurs. Attempts to stop him often resulted in penalties and Jazzy used to goad City's little supporters to fury by sarcastic references to Alan falling over in the penalty area. Scripture lessons were based on a book of extracts from the Bible. There was little explanation or discussion and we supported the periods as we supported all other periods whose relevance to life as we knew it was not immediately apparent.

Physics and Chemistry had now entered my life by courtesy of Messrs. Dollery and Stollery, generally known as Doolie and Stoolie. I didn't enjoy either subject. I was far happier watching Mr. Dollery playing cricket for the Lindum. A fine leg-break bowler and a useful bat, he was the elder brother of Horace, who played for Warwickshire and became their first professional captain. Mr. Stollery was a capable musician, played the organ and loved the music of Bach, so we had a common interest – it wasn't physics.

My only success that year was English. I had graduated from the Magnet and the Gem to detective stories, and read them at the rate of one every two or three days. In view of my dreadful reports, my parents were outraged, and threatened to forbid me to go to the Public Library for books. To them, my passion for G. K. Chesterton, R. A. Freeman, Anthony Berkeley, Agatha Christie, Dorothy Sayers, Freeman Wills Crofts, G. D. and M. Cole, was incomprehensible. My father had a look at 'Malice Aforethought' by Francis Iles and was scandalised. In a deleriously funny episode, he tried to explain why I shouldn't read it,

~ He tried to explain why I shouldn't read it ~

without doing so. All this reading meant I spelt, punctuated and wrote fluently without much effort. I had a large vocabulary and was seldom at a loss for a word. It did me nothing but good. It didn't, however, solve the rest of my problems, and exams. at the end of the summer term were a disaster. I was informed that I would be relegated to the slow stream and next year would be in 5c. My pride was hurt. I was quite unable to recognise that salvation was at hand, but traditionally the darkest hour is before the dawn.

The next year the pressure was off and my academic fortunes began to revive. Chance words can have an effect out of all proportion to their limited intent. "You'll get a credit in English", said John Phillips, pleased with a piece of work he was handing back to me. Good heavens! Such a consummation, however devoutly wished, was beyond my hopes, leave alone expectations. But if true, and he was apparently serious, might there be other areas of possible future success, and, if so, which? I had no idea what job I should like to have, my parents proposed banking as safe and respectable, though privately I could not see myself in that role. Success, however, is a powerful motivator and soon most subjects were going nicely.

For the first time, I was taught by Mr. Young, who took us once a week for essay writing. We wrote essays for him every weekend, but it was work I enjoyed and did better than any other. The masters began to seem more like human beings. I enjoyed Chick Adams' history lessons. He could be very kind and helpful. Times were hard in the thirties and one boy chosen for the first eleven had no way of buying white flannels. The matter was mentioned to Chick who loaned him his own pair for the season. The lad eventually became a group captain in the R.A.F. I once put my foot in it monumentally. I was late for afternoon school – a most rare occurrence – the class was working diligently, but Chick was not in evidence. I thought he had gone back to the Common Room to fetch a book. "Where's Chick?" I enquired. Too late I saw him sitting in a boy's desk, correcting his essay. "I'm here", he boomed to the ill-suppressed merriment of my class-mates. No more than six inches high, I crawled to my desk.

This year, too, I came to appreciate Mr. Williams, known as Weary from the characters in Comic Cuts (Weary Willie and Tired Tim). I don't think he was a good teacher of geography, but he took a genuine interest in people, the halt and the lame as well as the fleet of foot. We came to school on the same road and would walk companionably along together discussing our little world. He was a wise pastor and very kind in his judgements. I was beginning to have a few friends outside the choir and by the end of the year contemplating release from Cathedral duties. Success in School Certificate was vital and I didn't see how I could achieve this unless I had eighteen months before I took the exam. in which I could concentrate on that and that alone.

VIII

At Christmas 1933 I achieved my objective, convincing Dr. Slater that my time of usefulness was at an end. I blush to say that not all the cracking sounds in my voice were genuine, but I felt my future was at stake. Life in 5A was pretty good. I was on top of my work, making friends rapidly, games being very helpful, and able at last to take some part in the life of the school. Mr. Axton had gained promotion and for French this year I had a Mr. Shepherd, who had just arrived from University. In recent years we have become firm friends. I am much indebted to him for the help he gave me in my last years of teaching in setting up a Spanish department and teaching it, first to O, then to A. level. All this, however, lay many years in the future and Shep did not start teaching Spanish for another year. It never occurred to me to take advantage of the opportunity to learn it. No one explained what a valuable and pleasant language it is, and advice about courses of study was minimal. I would have liked to learn German, but it was not taught.

We still did woodwork, at which I was useless and must have caused Bill Bailey much frustration. Art was not taught after the second year to my regret. The Art Master, Mr. Hayes, was a fierce disciplinarian, but very approachable on a one-to-one basis. We had common interests in music and cricket. He was a Worcestershire man and would talk about Reg Perks by the hour. He also taught at the College of Art, where he formed and conducted an orchestra. Basil Pearce and I used to go to his concerts.

He had succeeded Mr. Hackford, an elderly man, whose life in school could only have been a foretaste of hell. He could not control his classes at all and unhappily the young are quite without mercy in such a situation. 'Take a thousand lines', he would scream, beside himself with fury, a pointless gesture since he would never collect them. I still remember his taking a metal beetle from a lad in my form and jumping up and down on it in a frenzy, but even at the time I wasn't so sure that it was as funny as it seemed. In the form above me were some notably lively characters who used to lock the smallest lads in the form in the toolchests. "Sir! Sir! Smith has disappeared! We can't find him anywhere!" "Then look for him boys, look for him!" This was the signal for them to seize brooms and energetically sweep up everything in sight. "What are you doing sitting on the floor, Richardson? Mr. Hackford has asked us to tidy the place up". The unwary soon found themselves deposited in the litter bin.

Lessons were enlivened by fierce political discussions. Most of the staff were Tory or Liberal, but one or two had left-wing sympathies, so it was quite interesting for a time, though eventually I felt I had heard it all before. My father was of the 'It's no use giving them decent houses, they'll only keep the coal in the bath' school of thought. I reacted against this strongly, becoming conscious of how dreadful some people's lives were. At the same time I was sceptical of the solutions offered by the left. In 1934 the clouds of war were no bigger than a man's hand, but this was the briefest of lulls before the storm.

School games from 3.30 till 5.00 were compulsory twice a week. We were divided into sets and left to get on with it. A master looked after the 1st XI and U.14, the remainder were controlled after a fashion by one member of staff who wandered about the field. I enjoyed football, though I was limited by lack of speed and bite in the tackle. I played for the best of all reasons – it was fun. I was interested in it, reasonably knowledgeable about tactics and in my last three years coached the U.14 under John Phillips' supervision. It was all very enjoyable and I learnt a lot from him. In my final year the team was Ray Dring, Willie Miller, Walter Groves, Stan Bruce, Roland Hayes, Harry Potterton, Algy Linnell, John Houle, Bernard Bowler, Eddie Dwane, Sid Blackbourn. Ray Dring gained an England cap, a great thrill to us all. Walter and Bernard were both right-footed. They were determined to be completely two-footed, and on nights when there was not a practice, they used to ask to borrow a ball and would go behind the goal and kick it into the net with their weaker foot so that it rolled back to them, for a whole hour. Within a year they were equally good with either foot, a fine example to any little lad. Our last two games were stiff ones, both away. We beat Carre's 9-4 at Sleaford, and King Edward's 8-3 at Sheffield. They really were a superb side.

Athletics were held at the end of the Lent Term, often in near freezing conditions. I was no performer and bored stiff most of the time, interest being momentarily awakened by the performances of my friends. Messrs. Dollery and Plant both had stopwatches, but they hardly ever agreed! In my last years, as a House Captain, I performed the only service I was capable of, getting others to take part, reserving my personal efforts for the five-mile cross country. The cross-country course, so far as I can remember, turned right out of School, along Wragby Road, left into Queensway, left again into Greetwell Road, right down to the end of Monks Road, then very sharp back left up steep fields to the Greetwell Road and across the farm tracks to Bunkers Hill, then sharp back through the ironstone workings to the Greetwell Road end, along Outer Circle Drive, down Wragby Road back to School. The killing bits were the long drag up the steep fields from Monks Road, and, worst of all, the ironstone mine area, a sea of mud more than ankle deep in wet weather. It was no unusual thing for a lad to lose a shoe beyond recovery in the mud and limp home as best he could. I did experience

~ and limp home as best he could ~

patriotic feelings of a mild kind when the Triangular Athletics Tournament with Newark and Retford took place, but I was glad when we could get back to serious business, which, as far as I was concerned, was football and cricket.

Swimming took place in a small open-air pool. P.E. periods were given over to it sometimes in the summer and then it was compulsory. The pool was agonisingly cold, and although I did finally learn to swim, I was never very good at it and reduced to admiring the fortitude of my friends who raced to and fro in its icy depths. On one occasion Footitt[2] (Joey) pushed in Mr. Phillips who was bathing at the time. Unfortunately for him, J.P.'s reactions were very quick and as he fell, he grabbed hold of Footitt and pulled him in fully dressed.

We were able to use the two hard tennis courts once we had reached the sixth form and I would often go back for a game in the summer evenings. We played doubles all the time and I enjoyed it very much in an undistinguished way. If not quite a team game, it was the next best thing.

I seem to remember playing tennis in the summer more than doing homework and fear this was because I spent more time playing than I should. I wonder sometimes how I got it done and managed to pass exams.

We had a fives court and played in the dinner hour and after school. I played reasonably well and liked the game very much, but, alas, even with gloves, my hands suffered terribly and I wisely gave it up before serious harm befell me.

Cricket was the one game where I could hope to achieve success and get my 1st XI colours. The annual all-day match against the Lincolnshire Gentlemen was eagerly awaited, as was the Speech Day match against the Old Boys and the game against the Masters. We had an excellent square to play on, attended devotedly by Albert Kent. He was prone to the normal groundsman syndrome of grumbling, but he was kind and helpful when he got to know you. He was a fine left-back, and his team, Burton Road, of which he was skipper, won the Lincoln League in 1936. The outfield was fast and rather bumpy, but the setting was lovely, the School capped by the clocktower on one side, handsome trees on the others. We had no sightscreens and the trees made it difficult at times to sight the ball. There were no worthwhile pitches off the square, but the second field had two grass nets and one concrete one. In the summer the professional, Mr. Widdowson, gave coaching there, and those who were keen were often allowed to go as an alternative to a P.E. lesson. He lived in Nottingham, came over by train each day, walked from St. Mark's station up to the School and back again in the evening. He was well over sixty at the time so it was a tiring day for him.

Those who gained their colours had a special white cricket cap, with a blue ribbon round the back and a small badge on the front. A large colours badge was worn on the blazer. I played under three captains, Geoff. Parkes, son of the manager of Lincoln City F.C., Paul Fox and Frank Arscott. I remember one occasion when Nottingham High School, frustrated beyond endurance by Paul's stout efforts to achieve a draw — he had scored only twenty in two hours — bowled the last over to him underhand. He solemnly returned each ball to the bowler.

I played in the House cricket team in 1934 and got as far as the fringe of the School First XI, though I did not finally make the team till two years later. Mr. Williams started an U.15 cricket team and asked me if I would like to umpire for them. I accepted with alacrity. Eric Shaw, who later played with distinction for Lincolnshire in the Minor Counties Competition, was a member of that team. One game was at Grantham and had anyone told me that in the fulness of time I would become Head of the Lower School at The King's School, I should have thought him out of his mind.

During this year I had tentatively thought of entering the Church. I was undoubtedly influenced by Mr. Barber, the curate of St. Nicholas, but I was also beginning to develop a social conscience, and feeling I would like to work in the slums. The idea grew, I talked to the Chancellor of the Cathedral, Dr. Srawley, who was in charge of candidates for the ministry, and asked those who taught me what the likelihood of School Certificate, and greatly daring, Higher Certificate, were. The response was very favourable, but there was a snag. I would need London Matriculation, or exemption from it, by gaining five credits in the School Certificate, one of which had to be Latin, which I hadn't done for four years. I would therefore have to go to RC (Remove Classical) next year and somehow achieve the necessary standard in one year, a forbidding prospect.

So September 1934 found me in RC, where for the first time I met Mr. Baxter, known to all as Jab from his initials. A prodigious worker, a fine teacher, immensely conscientious, he spared no efforts to help me in the next three years. Short, stout, with pincenez glasses, a Methodist

~ Short, stout with pincenez glasses ~

from Yorkshire, possessing a sharp temper and a fine sense of humour, he was a super schoolmaster. He also took us for English. I enjoyed the essay writing, but had no great love of the book of extracts from Cobbett's writings which was one of our set books. His meticulous dissection of Macbeth, based upon the insights of Bradley's Shakespearean Tragedy, opened my ideas to indepth critical study and its riches. Chick Adams' preparation for History, nineteenth century English and European, was a model of its kind, in the sense that if you knew his notes you got a good pass. Looking back on it, though, I feel we wasted much valuable time copying notes which he wrote up on the blackboard. They could easily have been duplicated, thus leaving more time for discussion and understanding.

In the previous summer exams. I had made a stupid error which had alarming results. I had done quite well in maths. and was promptly drafted into the top set which did Higher Maths. For Trig., Calculus and the like, I had neither aptitude or desire. I was very worried indeed that with no practice I would fail the ordinary maths. paper, an obligatory subject for Matric., and it took me fully two terms to convince 'Goot', Mr. Smith, that I must abandon it and secure my base by working through a pile of past papers.

I had by now decided that I would like to go to London University. Jab talked to me about Oxbridge, but I wanted London because if I lived there I should be able to spend quite a lot of my spare time doing social work and learning about big city conditions in the sort of area where I was considering work. In any case, there seemed no way of getting the extra money I would need at Oxbridge. I would take London Intermediate B.A. instead of Higher School Certificate, thereby having all three years at King's College, London for my degree course. Latin was obligatory, English an obvious choice, French and History providing the other two of the four subjects needed. I was on my fifth French teacher in five years, Mr. Wood, nicknamed Bosky, the sixth form master, a forbidding figure of whom even sixth formers were wary, if not slightly afraid. Years later, I learned that he had been on the short list for The King's School, Grantham! He was, I feel, a disappointed and ambitious man, who had very much wanted a headship. His marking was meticulously done, but several of my contemporaries have told me that his hard, cold, attitude, contributed considerably to their abandonment of sixth form study.

But all my work was going well, except Physics at which I had ceased to work seriously. I shouldn't want it in the sixth form and something had to go to accommodate all the extra work needed in Latin. Amusingly, two days before the School Certificate paper I had a qualm of conscience, went through previous papers, selected two questions which I reckoned were due to come up in the practical exam., and learned them up, complete with model results. They both did, I got 80% and, with the aid of two borderline theory papers, duly managed a credit to Mr. Stollery's amazement. Academically I was encouraged all through the year by the fact that, the previous year, Neville Richardson, a close friend in the choir, had gained five credits and exemption from London Matric., the first choirboy to do so. 'If I can do it, you can,' he told me and I began to think it just could happen. In fact, Basil Pearce and I each got seven credits.

The house system was altered that year, and I found myself in Pownall House with J. A. B. as housemaster. He was a good housemaster, watched all our matches, talked to his senior boys about house affairs, but gave them full responsibility. I played games on the school field most nights after school and acted as linesman for the U.14 football team. The Cathedral ceased to be responsible for my fees after I had gained my School Certificate, the letter of the law being firmly applied, but Mr. Young at once arranged for me to be a 'scholarship boy', albeit rather late in life!

"Would you care for some potatoes, Major Clarke?"

IX

I returned from a summer holiday in Torquay to enter the sixth form, with another little milestone passed. I had learnt to swim. Two years of very hard work lay ahead, since the failure rate for external Inter candidates was 67% and most of those taking the exam. were first year students at universities, which, in those days, could not award their own degrees but entered for external London degrees. There were just two of us doing 'Inter', Paul Fox and myself. Paul was captain of both cricket and football and a fine games player. We became close friends, our work and sporting interests giving us much in common. In those days Paul was vehemently left-wing in opinion. One of my most blissful memories is of a discussion period in which, goaded beyond endurance by some Socratic utterance from Mr. Wood, he finally burst out, 'I can understand anyone being a true blue Tory or a red hot Socialist, what I can't understand is anyone being a wishy-washy Liberal!

We soon found problems in our work. The Latin was well covered. We were attached to the Higher Certificate classes for language work and set books, being taught by Mr. Young. Livy was bad enough, Horace totally impossible without a crib. I'm sure Mr. Young knew we used one. From time to time he inserted a delicate barb. 'Ah, you are taking the reading.... and emending.... to....' Right fools we felt. We also had to do a fair dollop of Roman History, but that was with J. A. B. in whom we had total confidence. I still have his notes and marvel at their clarity. French, likewise, was done with Higher Certificate classes and fortunately it was all language work, we didn't have to do any set books. English was inadequately catered for. Mr. Wood gave us one period a week and we had to work on our own the rest of the time. Set books were Shakespeare – Henry IV Part One and The Winter's Tale, Chaucer – The

Pardoner's Tale, Bunyan – Grace Abounding, Fielding – Joseph Andrews, Dryden – a book of extracts. Of the non-enjoyment of the Bunyan and Dryden, the less said, the better! I wasn't worried about English, though. I enjoyed it and found most of it straight forward.

Where we were nearly wrecked was History. We had to do European History from 1498 to 1900 and after a term it began to dawn on us that this was a period Chick Adams had not studied much. Our work was, by and large, unplanned and we also had to cope with an enormous source book which was treated like a Shakespeare play with context questions. Furthermore, Chick was in charge of the School football team and much preferred to spend his time discussing it with his captain. This was a nice skive at first, but it wasn't long before we became seriously worried and lessons provided the ridiculous spectacle of the teacher trying to discuss football and the pupils trying very hard to talk about work. Hilarious, perhaps, but not to us. We had to badger him to set us essays and to our bewilderment he brought in Lord Acton's Essays and read them to us.

Early in the summer term I played my first game for the school First XI against the Old Lincolnians. I arrived at the wicket with the score 81 for 5 and was too paralysed to score for a quarter of an hour. At the other end John Hayward was proceeding in classical majesty to a large score. Thanks to his kind words of encouragement, I made some runs, and we won, which we didn't often do against the Old Boys. I kept my place in the team, though with no great distinction, but I remember that, after losing six wickets for 38 the Masters, Len Kirby and I put on 42 and we managed to bowl them out.

When we returned in September I was appointed a prefect. There were only six of us, so the position was privileged and we had a small room to ourselves where Paul and I played table tennis when we couldn't concentrate any longer on our work. The power to slipper the recalcitrant had been removed some two years before, not that I felt deprived. I found lads did what I asked so long as I did so good-humouredly. In my last year I wrote a little poem for 'The Lincolnian', lightly based on the Policeman's Song in 'The Pirates of Penzance'.

When the schoolboy's not engaged, with great enjoyment,
  In maturing his felonious little plans,
  His capacity for innocent employment
  Is just as great as any honest man's.
Our feelings we with difficulty smother
  When prefectorial duty's to be done.
Ah, take one consideration with another
  A prefect's life is not a happy one.
When the enterprising schoolboy is not cribbing,
  Or occupied in any other crime,
He strongly deprecates the thought of fibbing,
  And wouldn't cheek a prefect if he'd time.

He weeds the garden, always helps his mother,
And runs errands for his father in the rain,
All, take one consideration with another,
A prefect's job is really quite a strain.

There was a School Magazine every term and the senior boys wrote the various parts. Mr. Williams was in overall charge, read the material conscientiously, but very seldom interfered. We did all our own proof-reading and made final arrangements for the printing with Gilbert Fry, an old boy of the school.

The School First XI was undefeated that term and well deserved the distinction. Paul had moved from centre-half to centre-forward and scored nine goals in a match against Boston Grammar School. Before a game he didn't shave for three days and took out his minidenture. He was a frightening sight and it must have been worth a goal a game at least. Eventually my house had to play his. Knowing just what he would do to our uncertain defence, I casually mentioned that I thought my shooting was improving and I proposed to play centre-forward. This was rightly considered most hilarious, but the bait was taken and Paul appeared at centre-half for the opposition. I spent most of that match flat on my back from a series of splendidly timed shoulder charges. Physical contact was never frowned upon by those who used to play against me. Such was the enjoyment derived from these atavistic goings-on, that it was not until ten minutes from time that Moss House realised that they hadn't scored any of the twelve goals they might reasonably have expected. Alas, there was no happy ending. They did get one five minutes from time, and finding myself unbelievably unattended in front of goal, I managed to get the ball over the bar from three yards out, a feat I had hither to considered impossible.

Meanwhile we were far from confident about our work, Latin being the main worry. I even made what was for me the supreme sacrifice of giving up cricket in early June. Just before my retirement, we played Captain Webb's XI and a very large man was two or three not out a lunch. We concocted a brilliant plan. 'Would you care for some potatoes, Major Clarke?' 'Another helping of trifle, Major?' 'More biscuits and cheese, Major?' He ate an enormous lunch and we were quite right. He just could not move after lunch. He didn't need to. He stood at one end and belted the ball all over Lincolnshire, making 135 not out. No one wanted to bowl at that end.

I didn't even bother to apply to King's College since I did not expect to pass first time, though I hoped to be able to do so the following year. We had to take the exam. at the University at Nottingham and I stayed there for the week with our elderly cricket professional, Mr. Widdowson. Surrounded by first year University students in the Great Hall, I was overwhelmed. I just couldn't see how I could do as well as them – they were all wearing gowns! There were no exams. on Thursday and I went to Trent Bridge where I saw Joe Hardstaff take 214 not out off Somerset. The next morning in the bus on the way to the University, I began to think that my preparation for one section of the history paper was thin. I had gambled on a question on Louis XIV, but suppose it didn't turn up? So I read the textbook chapter on Peter the Great three times. And lo! the question on Louis XIV was vile and I couldn't have answered it, yet there was a nice straightforward question on Peter the Great.

The end of term was sad because Paul was leaving to go to Nottingham University and Mr. Young had been appointed to the headship of Rossall. I knew I would miss him greatly. He treated us as gentlemen fit to be trusted until we proved incontrovertibly otherwise. His concern for us went far beyond lessons. He used to invite the prefects three or four at a time to dine with him. Which knife to use, what finger bowls were for, how to make polite conversation in the drawing room, it was all a considerable ordeal at first, but our awkwardness was charmed away and lessons of great value learned. I owe him very much, though he did once insult me greatly. I made what I thought was a weighty contribution to the topic under discussion in a general studies period. A sorrowing gaze was fixed upon me. 'Woodward, I think you were born middle-aged!

He was no cricketer, but at soccer he turned out against the school. In shorts rather more than knee length, he appeared a comic character, yet whether at full-back or in goal, no one seemed to be able to get past him, though he was then forty years of age. The Chairman of the Governors was Frank, later Sir Francis, Hill. He invited us to lunch with him at the Saracen's Head. We were soon at ease, and he charmed us with his wit and interest in what we were doing.

We were pretty naive. I remember Mr. Young saying to us about some arrangement we needed to make, 'Oh, well, use my phone'. We were in a right panic. We were seventeen and had never spoken to anyone on the phone and were terribly unsure of what to do. One of his dinner parties gave me one of the worst half-hours of my life. They had just got a new puppy, which was less than half-trained and no sooner had we adjourned to the drawing room after dinner than it misbehaved and was carried out by Mrs. Young at arm's length, dripping happily all over the carpet. The convention of those days was to pretend nothing at all had happened. Paul and I dared not look at each other or we would have exploded in unseemly merriment. No sooner had Mrs. Young returned than she upset her coffee all over her dress and fled in disarray to change it. We were sore pressed.

The outside world didn't impinge on us much. For one thing, only two or three boys in the School had ever been across the Channel, and lacking the immediacy of television, the rise of Hitler, Mussolini in Abyssinia, seemed remote. The Spanish Civil War was another matter and once the Axis powers poured men and material in to help France, many of us read the signs correctly and believed they were practising for

~ Dripping happily all over the carpet ~

war, and that scenes we saw on the news reels in the cinema would one day be part of our own experience.

In 1936, one summer's day, the air liner Hindenburg passed right over the School field at break. We watched it in amazement. It was unbelievably large and not very high up, so we had a splendid view. It cast a large shadow, a prophetic event.

One morning I was in the Secretary's office and Miss Footman said about a little lad who had just gone out, "I don't think that boy ever gets enough to eat". It just hadn't occurred to me that this could happen to anyone I knew. The world was never quite the same again.

I was beginning to learn about the outside world by reading the Manchester Guardian. I had come to it by discovering the cricket reports of Neville Cardus, which gave me enormous pleasure. I used to walk down to the Library most days in the summer for the sheer pleasure of reading them. Unhappily nobody wrote with such distinction about football, but I made fortnightly pilgrimages to Sincil Bank where Lincoln City played some football very enjoyable to watch, the idea being to score more goals than the other lot. Incredibly, the first time in my life that I saw Manchester United, City thrashed them 5-1. In those days a lad could go to a football match without any worries about violence – in that respect they were 'the good old days'.

One lad in School was the son of a tailor in the city who was nearly ruined by a rash promise to give a new hat to each member of the Lincoln

City team if they won a Cup match against illustrious opponents. The odds against their doing so were astronomical, but Cup games are notorious for upsetting the odds and a grinning team duly presented itself the following Monday. When he was in the fifth year the lad grew a moustache. Authority strangely took no notice of this aid to masculine beauty, but the opinion of his fellows was greatly offended by what was considered to be overweening pride and a bunch of them sat on him and removed half of it. Dickie was outraged and challenged the nearest

~ and removed half of it ~

aggressor to single and mortal combat. This was a very foolish thing to do since the shorn lamb was rotund and not very mobile and the other lad, Tim Macdonald, was a talented boxer. It was all very embarrassing, but the fight duly took place on the second field. Tim did just enough to discourage the challenger from going beyond a couple of rounds, wounded pride was satisfied and everyone was relieved it was all over.

One feature of Mr. Young's headship was the opening of the new buildings early in 1937. For the first time we had a gymnasium cum assembly hall, a sixth form room, geography room and art room. They made a fine addition to an already impressive range of buildings and the old army hut in the quad was removed, the playground considerably extended and proper bicycle stands provided. The buildings of 1906 had stood the test of time pretty well, were reasonably light and warm and good to work in. The caretaker, who must have worked for forty years at the school, was Jack Green. He was a young man when I was a pupil, perhaps inclined to a belief in the doctrine of original sin as far as small boys were concerned. I came to know him well in later years and to appreciate his excellent qualities.

The tiles in the cloister were an ugly brownish-yellow colour, but familiarity led to acceptance. The cloister provided shelter in wet weather when at the usual game of playground football were not possible in break and the tuckshop, over which Mr. Plant presided, was a scene of much activity. He was the Deputy Head, an unbending little figure, devoted to the School. It is a fact that one hapless parent arrived at school one day

The new buildings of Lincoln School, 1937.

and asked to speak to Mr. Shrubby. Unhappily, he was at pains to prevent his genuine interest in his pupils ever showing through and seemed to us to subscribe firmly to the philosophy of 'See what Johnnie is doing and tell him to stop it.'

When new changing rooms were built in 1937 we had showers for the first time. Younger boys had nowhere to wash after games, middle school had one or two washbasins and a small footbath, so this was a radical departure from tradition. After football we went home very inadequately cleaned up for most of the time I was at school and the filthy, mudspattered objects who limped in after crosscountry, looking

~ the filthy, mudspattered objects who limped in ~

like refugees from trench warfare in World War One, couldn't do much to repair the damage before pulling on their clothes and going home. As a small boy I did P.T. (when I couldn't get out of it!) in my school clothes with an ex-army S.M. With the arrival of Mr. Bailey we were made to change into football shirt and shorts and were not quite so disgustingly sweaty for the rest of the day.

Mr. Wood entered upon the new sixth-form room with great relish. It had a handsome floor of wooden blocks, which he insisted upon having polished at regular intervals by its unhappy inhabitants who greatly feared housemaid's knee. In the middle were tables where lessons were conducted, all round were bureau desks for each boy to work at when he was not being taught. It was an astonishly stupid arrangement, concentration on one's own work being well-nigh impossible when masters were taking a lesson in the middle of the room. He had one idea which was excellent. Penguin books had just come into being at sixpence a time. We all contributed our tanner and a stock for borrowing was kept in a little room next to the form room. I certainly had my sixpennyworth.

An interesting little area was the four tiny studies for the senior boarders. The coal fires burnt merrily in the winter and so did the toast sometimes. It was very pleasant to sit in a comfortable chair in John Hayward's room, discuss cricket and lesser school affairs after school hours, a delightful contrast to the impersonal surroundings among which we otherwise passed our days. I remember vividly my first meeting with Mr. Franklin, the day he came to be interviewed for the Headship. I backed out of John Hayward's room, still chattering away and trod heavily on his toe. I just hoped that, if appointed, he wouldn't recognise me next term.

X

In the summer holidays I went to Carlisle for a fortnight and, by means of two 'ten bob' tickets on the railway, was able to visit the Lakes, the Pennines and the Roman Wall. I climbed my first mountain, Great Gable, on a beautiful summer's day, and my love affair with mountains has continued ever since. In the evening I used to love to go on the little railway to Silloth and watch the sunset over the Solway, looking over to Criffel. I returned to find that I had passed Inter, my joy being only spoilt by learning that Paul had not and would have to retake the exam. at the end of his first year at Nottingham University.

Our new Head Master was Mr. Franklin and he accepted Mr. Young's recommendation that I should be Captain of the School. Delightful prospects now opened before me, a whole year's reading with no exam. pressures. I had already made up my mind to take an Honours degree in English, with French to pass degree standard. Mr. Wood superintended my reading and I learned to be at ease with him, which I wouldn't have believed possible two years before. He even helped me to make a beginning in learning to read Anglo-Saxon, we spent pleasant, relaxed periods together once a week, and I came to know a side of him very different from the one he usually presented to his pupils.

I got on well with the new Head Master and was often employed to try to teach his form French if he was delayed in the office at the start of a period!

My closest friend was now Ken Paulger. We were in the same House

Lincoln School 1st XI in 1938. Ken Paulger is sitting second from the left, I am sitting on the right.

and managed to win the House Shield that year. We weren't the strongest house, but we worked at it. Ken was a fine sprinter and played all games well. He was to have a distinguished career in the army and became a brigadier. Among the members of my house was a small boy who played outside right in the junior House team, made a notable effort in the cross-country race and whose enthusiastic approach to all he did was a joy to behold. He was a fine violinist and I had the pleasure of accompanying him in School concerts. Today, Neville Marriner is the Director of the Academy of St. Martin's in the Field, a specialist in music of the Baroque period, and whose recordings and television appearances have made him a national figure. Another lad who was to become well-known in the world of music and television was Steve Race, but I must confess to being unable to remember much about him while he was at school and can only conclude he took little part in the life of the School.

Pour encourager les autres, I ran in the Five Mile cross-country. To my surprise I found I could lumber on at a modest but unflinching pace which would just about get me in the first dozen. Ken won the Victor Ludorum and Norman Cass was a tower of strength in most sports. That, and some enthusiastic juniors, meant that we did quite well in everything and was the reason for our winning the House Shield.

At Easter I stayed with my aunt in London and prospected for lodgings, armed with the University's list of recommended lodgings. I had been accepted without even an interview on the strength of my pass in Inter and the School's testimonial. All ended happily at 32, North Side, Clapham Common.

~ I started the cricket season in fine style with the bat ~

I started the cricket season in fine style with the bat, making runs for the School and the Old Lincolnians. I was greatly looking forward to the visit of Jack Hobbs, who had promised to play in Captain Webb's XI, when, horror of horrors, I suddenly became ill. 'Appendicitis', said the doctor. After three days the surgeon said it was not necessary to operate, but I was very weak. I was determined to play, and did so, a fortnight later. I made 10, but my early season form had deserted me. I did finally gain my colours and still have the cap! I had the privilege of sitting opposite the great man at lunch and appreciating what a delightful person he was. Afterwards he bludgeoned the School bowlers all round the field in making 89. His timing was marvellous.

Deceptively suddenly the last day of term arrived. Of the moments of truth scattered throughout my decade at Lincoln School, one stood out. Even today, I remember the sense of shock when Weary Williams told us at the age of twelve that we didn't come to school to learn lessons out of textbooks, so much as to learn to live together as people. My little conformist soul was outraged at such appalling betrayal from within, but now I know how right and wise he was.

It is not easy to reach a dispassionate judgement on one's school. To sail between the Scylla of 'the good old days' and the Charybdis of near-total condemnation would tax the seamanship of the most accomplished mariner and many would say it is a voyage best not attempted. Any institution has to be seen within the context of its times and must of necessity reflect many of the virtues and failings of the society of the day. Society was class-conscious and so was the School, but this faded away as you progressed up the School until it reached vanishing point. There was little bureaucracy and some things were cheerfully casual. For instance, the first first division football match I saw was at Derby (they beat Wolves 5-0) and I was allowed to leave school at mid-day one Wednesday to go with another boy and his father to see the match. On the other hand, to be seen without a school cap was a heinous offence, staff and prefects alike exercising perpetual vigilance.

Did the School encourage hard work, enjoyment of learning and good personal relationships? Broadly speaking, yes. By the standards of today it was small, there were about three hundred boys in the main school when I left, and this made it easier to know and be known by staff and fellow pupils. Discipline was fairly strict and often pernickety. Punishments were frequent, lines rather than essays ('empty vessels make most sound' and similar banalities), detention on Saturday afternoon, the star system (one star – deleted at the end of the week, two stars – carried forward to the end of the following week, three stars – automatic Saturday detention, six stars – a whacking from the Head Master) and keeping-in after school. A few masters managed to bridge the gap between man and boy, most preferred to remain behind the defensive position of authority and were careful never to relax. Most had forgotten what it was like to be a boy and could not imaginatively enter into and appreciate the world of an eleven year old or a sixteen year old. But this was normal in the thirties and is still common today.

The curriculum had gaps which are obvious with the benefit of hindsight. There was no provision for the teaching of Biology, no German, and Spanish only in my last years at school, and then restricted to one or two interested boys in the sixth form. Economics and General Studies were also lacking, but discussion periods were often lively and varied in content. In common with most schools of the day, art and music were little regarded, lessons in these subjects not going beyond the second year.

Work was stimulated by fear of punishment in the lower forms and was frequently ordered to be rewritten, whether for untidiness or inadequacy. Blame was more frequent than praise, which was considered likely to go to the head, with evil results. Boys must be kept in their place was the watchword, though this changed markedly on entry into the sixth form. But the boy of eleven is just as much a person as the boy of sixteen and no less worthy of respect, understanding and concern. If you didn't know how to do work, you didn't like to ask because you were quite likely to be met by the sarcasm of a teacher and the scorn of brighter pupils. This simply led to cribbing as the easiest way of avoiding trouble and ultimately solved nothing. Some boys left before taking School Certificate, others left early in the Sixth Form, and many of these lads were good enough to achieve more academic success than they did, given encouragement. Schools in those days had no member of staff to give advice on careers, universities and jobs, but since this was well-nigh universal, most lads made their way in the end.

In spite of these flaws, which are easier to see now than fifty years ago, Lincoln School in the thirties was a pretty good place in which to grow up. It was comprehensive in a good way, in that boys from professional backgrounds and boys from poor homes learned to live together, appreciate one another's qualities and become firm friends. Academic success came with hard work and in the upper forms many of the forbidding figures in cap and gown (all masters wore a gown for teaching) emerged as human beings and a genuinely friendly relationship became possible. The School provided an environment in which qualities of leadership, honesty, and integrity could grow and develop, even if compassion was not so obvious. I owe much to those who taught me and retained the friendship of some of them for years.

Any teacher must of necessity imitate or react from those who taught him, and in different ways John Phillips, Jimmy Baxter, Maurice Williams and Harry Wood have influenced me throughout my teaching life. I have, however, enjoyed the friendship of pupils of all ages in a way that would not really have been possible in the thirties, and have found pleasure in talking naturally to eleven year olds as much as sixthformers and hardly ever found any lad seek to take advantage of this.

I have, too, tried very hard to create a climate of opinion in which a

Summer 1979, just before retirement as Head of Lower School at the King's School Grantham. *Photo:* Grantham Journal

boy who did not understand anything would think it natural to ask. I never called cribbing a crime or punished it, and it was very rare. I simply called it unnecessary and stupid, since, if a lad didn't understand, all he had to do was to ask and I would explain it. In my latter years I taught languages, Spanish to A. Level, German to O. Level and sometimes Italian to O. Level, in all of which I was self taught. This helped me enormously for I was always in a learning situation myself, struggling with Russian or something else, and was therefore only too conscious of the difficulties my pupils were encountering, since I was continually meeting difficulties myself. In these days there is far more pastoral work, due to broken homes, the pressures of affluence, high qualifications for careers, and living in a violent society. As Head of Lower School I tried never to be too busy to see any boy who wanted to talk to me about his problems. I knew them all by their Christian names from the age of eleven, also out of the question in the thirties, and we could talk as one human being to another.

The foundations of my approach to a life of teaching were laid by those who taught me at Lincoln School. I simply tried to find a method suitable to the age and society in which I worked. I am happy to record my gratitude to those who taught me, and to pay this affectionate tribute to my native city.